ACTIVITY WORKBOOK

SIDE by SIDE

3

Extra

Steven J. Molinsky
Bill Bliss

with
Carolyn Graham

Contributing Authors
Elizabeth Handley • Dorothy Lynde

Illustrated by
Richard E. Hill

Side by Side Extra Activity Workbook 3

Pearson Education, 10 Bank Street, White Plains, NY 10606

Staff credits: The people who make up the *Side by Side Extra* team, representing content creation, design, manufacturing, marketing, multimedia, project management, publishing, rights management, and testing are Pietro Alongi, Allen Ascher, Rhea Banker, Elizabeth Barker, Lisa Bayrasli, Elizabeth Carlson, Jennifer Castro, Tracey Munz Cataldo, Diane Cipollone, Aerin Csigay, Victoria Denkus, Dave Dickey, Daniel Dwyer, Wanda España, Oliva Fernandez, Warren Fischbach, Pam Fishman, Nancy Flaggman, Patrice Fraccio, Irene Frankel, Aliza Greenblatt, Lester Holmes, Leslie Johnson, Janet Johnston, Caroline Kasterine, Barry Katzen, Ray Keating, Renee Langan, Jaime Lieber, José Antonio Méndez, Julie Molnar, Alison Pei, Pamela Pia, Stuart Radcliffe, Jennifer Raspiller, Kriston Reinmuth, Mary Perrotta Rich, Tania Saiz-Sousa, Katherine Sullivan, Paula Van Ells, Kenneth Volcjak, Paula Williams, and Wendy Wolf.

Text composition: TSI Graphics, Inc.

Illustrations: Richard E. Hill

The authors gratefully acknowledge the contribution of Tina Carver in the development of the original *Side by Side* program.

ISBN-10: 0-13-245987-6
ISBN-13: 978-0-13-245987-7

Printed in the United States of America

1 2 3 4 5 6 7 8 9 10—V011—23 22 21 20 19 18 17 16

CONTENTS

A WHAT'S HAPPENING?

what	bake	cook	move	sit
where	compose	go	read	watch

STUDENT BOOK
PAGES **1–10**

1. A. ___What's___ Fran ___reading___?

   B. ___She's reading___ her e-mail.

3. A. _____ Nancy _____?

   B. _____ a game show.

5. A. _____ you and your wife

   _____?

   B. _____ to Miami.

7. A. _____ Victor _____?

   B. _____ a symphony.

2. A. ___Where's___ Fred _____?

   B. _____ to the clinic.

4. A. _____ you _____?

   B. _____ dinner.

6. A. _____ your grandmother

   and grandfather _____?

   B. _____ in the park.

8. A. _____ you _____?

   B. _____ an apple pie.

2   Activity Workbook

1.

A. Hi. What _____are_____ you doing?

B. _____I'm watching_____ a movie on TV.

A. Oh. I don't want to disturb you. _____ Anna busy?

B. Yes, _____. _____ a bath.

A. I'll call back later.

2.

A. Hi, Bill. _____ the children okay?

B. Yes. _____ fine.

A. What _____ doing?

B. Vicky _____ her homework, and

Timmy _____ baseball in the yard.

A. How about you? _____ doing?

B. _____ dinner for you and the kids.

A. I'll be home soon.

3.

A. Hello, Peter. This is Mr. Taylor. _____ your father at home?

B. No, _____. _____ at the health club.

A. Can I speak to your mother?

B. I'm sorry. _____ busy right now. _____ the washing machine. It's broken.

A. Okay. I'll call back later.

4.

A. Hello, ... Can I speak to ....?

B. I'm sorry. ....

A. Well, can I speak to ....?

B. I'm afraid ....

A. Okay. I'll call back later.

C YOU DECIDE: *Why Is Today Different?*

1. *(clean)* I never _____clean_____ my apartment, but _____I'm cleaning_____ it today

   because __my grandmother is going to visit me *(or)* my boss is coming over for dinner__ .

2. *(iron)* Roger never _____ his shirts, but _____ them today

   because _____ .

3. *(argue)* We never _____ with our landlord, but _____ with him today

   because _____ .

4. *(worry)* I never _____ about anything, but _____ today because

   _____ .

5. *(watch)* Betty never _____ the news, but _____ it today because

   _____ .

6. *(write)* Uncle Phil never _____ to us, but _____ to us today

   because _____ .

7. *(take)* I never _____ the bus, but _____ it today because

   _____ .

8. *(comb)* My son never _____ his hair, but _____ it today

   because _____ .

9. *(get up)* My daughter never _____ early, but _____ early today

   because _____ .

10. *(smile)* Mr. Grimes never _____, but _____ today because

    _____ .

11. *(bark)* Our dogs never _____, but _____ today

    because _____ .

12. *(wear)* Alice never _____ perfume, but _____ it today

    because _____ .

D WHAT ARE THEY SAYING?

1. I recommend the fish.

   Do you recommend the chicken, too?

2. My husband bakes delicious cakes.

   _____ he _____ pies, too?

3. My daughter gets up early.

   _____ your son _____ early, too?

4. They always complain about the traffic.

   _____ they _____ about the weather, too?

5. Maria speaks Italian and Spanish.

   _____ she _____ French, too?

6. My grandson lives in Miami.

   _____ your granddaughter _____ there, too?

7. I watch the news every morning.

   _____ every evening, too?

8. My sister plays soccer.

   _____ tennis, too?

9. Robert practices the trombone at night.

   _____ during the day, too?

10. We plant vegetables every year.

    _____ flowers, too?

11. Stanley always adds salt to the stew.

    _____ pepper, too?

12. I always wear a jacket to work.

    _____ a tie, too?

13. My cousin Sue rides a motorcycle.

    _____ a bicycle, too?

14. My grandfather jogs every day.

    _____ when it rains?

15. We need bread from the supermarket.

    _____ milk, too?

16. Gregory always irons his shirts.

    _____ his pants, too?

17. Our neighbors have three dogs.

    _____ any cats?

Across

3. I like to cook. I'm an excellent _____.
4. I can type. I'm a very good _____.
5. Sally swims fast. She's a fast _____.
6. Jeff likes to play sports. He's a good _____.
7. My sons drive taxis. They're both taxi _____.

Down

1. You ski well. You're a very good _____.
2. We act in plays and movies. We're ____.
5. My children love to skate. They're wonderful _____.

F WHAT'S THE ANSWER?

Circle the correct answer.

1. Does Hector like to play tennis?
   a. Yes, he likes.
   b. Yes, he does.
   c. Yes, he is.

2. Are you a graceful dancer?
   a. No, I don't.
   b. No, you aren't.
   c. No, I'm not.

3. Does your boss work hard?
   a. Yes, he is.
   b. Yes, he does.
   c. Yes, he works.

4. Is the food at this restaurant spicy?
   a. Yes, it isn't.
   b. Yes, it does.
   c. Yes, it is.

5. Are your children good athletes?
   a. Yes, I am.
   b. Yes, they are.
   c. Yes, they do.

6. Do you and your girlfriend like to cook?
   a. Yes, she does.
   b. Yes, they do.
   c. Yes, we do.

7. Am I a good teacher?
   a. Yes, you are.
   b. Yes, he is.
   c. Yes, you do.

8. Does your husband send e-mail messages to you?
   a. Yes, he is.
   b. Yes, he does.
   c. Yes, she does.

WHAT ARE THEY SAYING?

1. A. I ____don't____ like to eat at Albert's house because he _____ cook very well.

   B. I know. Everybody says he _____ a very good _____.

2. A. I know you _____ like to drive with me because you think _____ a terrible driver.

   B. That's not true. I think you _____ very carefully!

3. A. _____ like to type?

   B. No, I _____. _____ not a very accurate typist.

   A. I disagree. _____ an accurate typist, but you _____ very slowly.

4. A. Oliver Jones is an excellent composer.

   B. I agree. He _____ beautifully. I think _____ very talented.

5. A. Irene _____ going swimming with us today because she _____ like to swim when it's cold.

   B. That's too bad. I really like to go swimming with her. She's a very good _____.

6. A. I'm jealous of my classmates. They speak English very well, and I _____.

   B. That's not true. Your classmates _____ English clearly, but you're a good English _____, too.

H **LISTENING**

Listen to each question and then complete the answer.

1. Yes, ____he does____.
2. No, ____she isn't____.
3. Yes, _____.
4. Yes, _____.
5. No, _____.

6. Yes, _____.
7. No, _____.
8. Yes, _____.
9. No, _____.
10. Yes, _____.

11. No, _____.
12. Yes, _____.
13. Yes, _____.
14. No, _____.
15. No, _____.

GRAMMARRAP: *Does He Like the Movies?*

Listen. Then clap and practice.

A. Does he like   the movies?

B.   No,   he doesn't.   He likes   TV.

A. Does she like   the mountains?

B.   No,   she doesn't.   She likes   the sea.

A. Do you like to   hike?

B.   No,   I don't.   I like to   dive.

A. Do they like to   walk?

B.   No,   they don't.   They like to   drive.

A. Is he studying   music?

B.   No,   he isn't.   He's studying   math.

A. Is she taking   a shower?

B.   No,   she isn't.   She's taking   a bath.

A. Are they living   in Brooklyn?

B.   No,   they aren't. They're living   in Queens.

A. Are you washing   your shirt?

B.   No,   I'm not.   I'm washing   my jeans.

WHAT'S THE QUESTION?

1. We're waiting for <u>the bus</u>. ___What are you waiting for?___

2. He's thinking about <u>his girlfriend</u>. ___Who is he thinking about?___

3. They're ironing <u>their shirts</u>. _____

4. I'm calling <u>my landlord</u>. _____

5. She's dancing with <u>her father</u>. _____

6. He's watching <u>the news</u>. _____

7. They're complaining about <u>the rent</u>. _____

8. She's playing baseball with <u>her son</u>. _____

9. They're visiting <u>their cousins</u>. _____

10. We're looking at <u>the animals in the zoo</u>. _____

11. I'm writing about <u>my favorite movie</u>. _____

12. He's arguing with <u>his boss</u>. _____

13. She's knitting a sweater for <u>her daughter</u>. _____

14. We're making <u>pancakes</u>. _____

15. I'm sending an e-mail to <u>my uncle</u>. _____

16. They're worrying about <u>their examination</u>. _____

17. She's talking to <u>the soccer coach</u>. _____

18. He's skating with <u>his grandparents</u>. _____

1. A.   Where are you and your husband taking ____your____ children?

    B.   __We're__ taking ___them___ to the zoo.

2. A.   Why is Richard calling all _____ friends today?

    B.   _____ wants to tell _____ about _____ new car.

3. A.   What are your parents going to give you for your birthday?

    B.   I'm not sure, but _____ might give _____ a puppy.

4. A.   Why is Susie visiting _____ grandparents?

    B.   _____ wants to show _____ her new bicycle.

5. A.   Why are you wearing a safety helmet on _____ head?

    B.   _____ don't want to hurt _____ head while I'm skateboarding.

6. A.   Where are you taking _____ new girlfriend on Saturday night?

    B.   _____ taking _____ to see the new science fiction movie downtown.

7. A.   Why are those students complaining about their teacher?

    B.   _____ think she gives _____ too much homework.

8. A.   Can I tell you and Dad about the party now?

    B.   No. We're sleeping now. You can tell _____ about _____ tomorrow morning.

9. A.   Why is Mrs. Jenkins waiting for the plumber?

    B.   The sink is leaking. Charlie, the plumber, says _____ can fix _____.

10. A.   Timmy, why are you arguing with _____ sister?

    B.   _____ wants to play with _____ new toys, but she can't. They're mine.

L WHAT'S THE WORD?

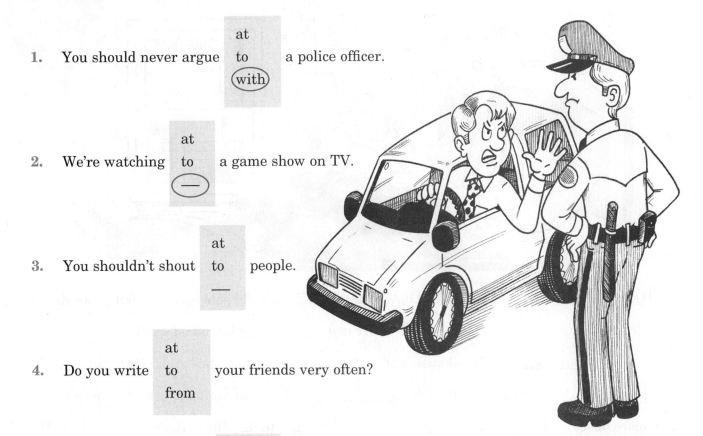

1. You should never argue
   at
   to
   (with) a police officer.

2. We're watching
   at
   to
   (—) a game show on TV.

3. You shouldn't shout
   at
   to
   — people.

4. Do you write
   at
   to
   from your friends very often?

5. They always complain
   at
   —
   about the weather.

6. We visit
   at
   to
   — our sister's friends in Texas once a year.

7. I'm helping
   at
   to
   — my neighbors
   to
   with
   — their garden.

8. I'm always frustrated when I have to wait
   for
   —
   at the bus.

9. Call
   to
   —
   at the exterminator right away!

Herbert *(have)* ___had ¹ a very bad day yesterday. He usually gets up early, but yesterday morning he *(get up)* _____ ² very late! He *(eat)* _____ ³ breakfast quickly, *(rush)* _____ ⁴ out of the house, and *(run)* _____ ⁵ to the bus stop. Unfortunately, he *(miss)* _____ ⁶ the bus. He *(wait)* _____ ⁷ for ten minutes, but there weren't any more buses, so he *(decide)* _____ ⁸ to walk to his office. Herbert was upset. He *(arrive)* _____ ⁹ at work two and a half hours late!

Herbert *(sit)* _____ ¹⁰ down at his desk and *(begin)* _____ ¹¹ his work. He *(call)* _____ ¹² a few people on the telephone, and he *(type)* _____ ¹³ a few letters. But he was in a hurry, and he *(make)* _____ ¹⁴ a lot of mistakes. He *(fix)* _____ ¹⁵ the mistakes, but when he *(finish)* _____ ¹⁶ the letters and *(put)* _____ ¹⁷ them on his desk, he *(spill)* _____ ¹⁸ water all over them.

At noon, Herbert *(go)* _____ ¹⁹ to the company cafeteria and *(order)* _____ ²⁰ a pizza for lunch. That was a big mistake. The pizza was very spicy, and Herbert *(feel)* _____ ²¹ sick for the rest of the day.

Herbert's afternoon was even worse than his morning. He *(forget)* _____ ²² about an important meeting, his computer *(crash)* _____ ²³, he *(fall)* _____ ²⁴ asleep at his desk, his chair *(break)* _____ ²⁵, and he *(hurt)* _____ ²⁶ his arm.

Herbert *(leave)* _____ ²⁷ the office at 5:00, *(take)* _____ ²⁸ the bus home, and immediately *(go)* _____ ²⁹ to bed! What a terrible, terrible day!

B LISTENING

Listen and circle the correct answer.

1. yesterday
   (every day)

2. (yesterday)
   every day

3. yesterday
   every day

4. yesterday
   every day

5. yesterday
   every day

6. yesterday
   every day

7. yesterday
   every day

8. yesterday
   every day

9. yesterday
   every day

10. yesterday
    every day

11. yesterday
    every day

12. yesterday
    every day

C WHAT'S THE WORD?

Fill in the missing words. Then read the story aloud.

| decide | lift | need | paint | plant | roller-blade | wait | want |

Last Saturday everyone __wanted__¹ my help. In the morning, I

_____² heavy furniture for my wife, and I _____³ the

bathroom walls. Then I _____⁴ in the park with my son and

_____⁵ flowers with my daughter. In the afternoon, my brother

_____⁶ my help. I went to a store with him and _____⁷

while he _____⁸ which suit to buy for his wedding.

D PUZZLE: *What Did They Do?*

Across

2. ride
3. teach
5. are
6. meet
7. deliver

Down

1. write
4. get
5. work

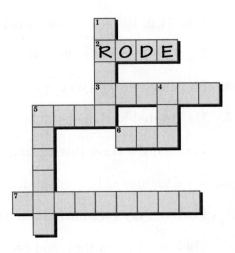

WHAT'S THE QUESTION?

1. _____Did you buy_____ the green one?   No, I didn't. I bought the blue one.

2. _____ a plane?   No, they didn't. They took a boat.

3. _____ a movie?   No, she didn't. She saw a play.

4. _____ French?   No, he didn't. He spoke Arabic.

5. _____ your arm?   No, I didn't. I broke my leg.

6. _____ at seven?   No, it didn't. It began at eight.

7. _____ to Paris?   No, she didn't. She flew to Rome.

8. _____ the beef?   No, we didn't. We had the chicken.

9. _____ with you?   No, they didn't. They went alone.

10. _____ too softly?   No, you didn't. You sang too loudly.

11. _____ your mother?   No, he didn't. He met my father.

12. _____ your keys?   No, I didn't. I lost my ring.

F **WHAT'S THE ANSWER?**

was	were
wasn't	weren't

angry	hungry	prepared	scared	tired
bored	on time	sad	thirsty	

1. The students fell asleep in Professor Winter's class because _____they were bored_____.

2. I didn't finish my sandwich today because _____I wasn't hungry_____.

3. They went to bed early last night because _____.

4. She didn't do well on the test because _____.

5. He shouted at them because _____.

6. I missed the train this morning because _____.

7. My daughter didn't finish all her milk because _____.

8. I covered my eyes during the movie because _____.

9. They cried when they said good-bye at the airport because _____.

SOMETHING DIFFERENT

1. Albert usually drives very carefully.

   He ____didn't drive____ carefully yesterday afternoon.

   He _____drove_____ much too fast.

2. Alice usually comes home from work early.

   She _____ home early last night.

   She _____ home late.

3. I usually take the bus to work.

   I _____ the bus this morning.

   I _____ the train.

4. We usually go to the movies on Saturday.

   We _____ to the movies last Saturday.

   We _____ to a concert.

5. Carl and Tom usually forget their homework.

   They _____ their homework yesterday.

   They _____ their lunch.

6. Mr. Tyler usually wears a suit to the office.

   He _____ a suit today.

   He _____ jeans.

7. Professor Hall usually teaches biology.

   She _____ biology last semester.

   She _____ astronomy.

8. Mr. and Mrs. Miller usually eat dinner at 7:00.

   They _____ dinner at 7:00 last night.

   They _____ at 9:00.

9. My grandmother usually gives me a tie for my birthday.

   She _____ me a tie this year.

   She _____ me a watch.

10. Alan usually sits by himself in English class.

    He _____ by himself today.

    He _____ with all his friends.

11. I usually have cereal for breakfast.

    I _____ cereal this morning.

    I _____ eggs.

12. Amanda usually sings very beautifully.

    She _____ beautifully last night.

    She _____ very badly.

1. A. _____Did you_____ clean your apartment this week?

   B. No, I ___didn't___. I ___was___ too lazy.

2. A. _____ meet the company president at the office party?

   B. No, we _____. But we

   _____ his wife.

3. A. _____ Richard fall?

   B. Yes, he _____. He skated

   very quickly, and he _____ very careful.

4. A. _____ Rita deliver all the pizzas today?

   B. No, _____. The people at

   10 Main Street _____ home.

5. A. _____ Roger _____ asleep at the meeting this morning?

   B. No, _____. But he

   _____ asleep later in his

   office. He _____ very tired.

6. A. _____ you ride your motorcycle to work today?

   B. No, _____. I _____

   my bicycle, and I _____ late.

   My supervisor _____ upset.

7. A. _____ like the movie?

B. Yes, I _____. It _____ great! How about you? Did you like it?

A. No, I _____. I thought it _____ boring.

8. A. _____ Mrs. Sanchez your Spanish teacher last semester?

B. Yes, she _____. _____ you in her class?

A. No, _____. I _____ take Spanish. I took French.

9. A. _____ you complain to your landlord about the problems in your apartment?

B. Yes, we _____. He listened to us, but he _____ fix anything. We _____ very angry.

10. A. _____ the students dance gracefully in the school play?

B. No, _____. They _____ very awkwardly. They _____ very nervous.

11. A. Dad, _____ you buy anything at the supermarket?

B. Yes, _____. I _____ some food for dinner.

A. _____ buy any ice cream?

B. Sorry. I _____. There _____ any.

12. A. Grandpa, _____ you a good soccer player when you _____ young?

B. Yes, _____. I _____ a very good player. I _____ fast, and I _____ clumsy.

1. How did Steven sprain his ankle? *(play tennis)*

   _____ He sprained his ankle while he was playing tennis. _____

2. How did your sister rip her pants? *(exercise)*

   _____

3. How did you break your arm? *(play volleyball)*

   _____

4. How did James poke himself in the eye? *(fix his sink)*

   _____

5. How did you and your brother hurt yourselves? *(skateboard)*

   _____

6. How did Mr. and Mrs. Davis trip and fall? *(dance)*

   _____

7. How did your father burn himself? *(cook french fries)*

   _____

8. How did your daughter get a black eye? *(fight with the kid across the street)*

   _____

9. How did you cut yourself? *(chop carrots)*

   _____

10. How did Robert lose his cell phone? *(jog in the park)*

    _____

11. How did you _____?

    _____

J GRAMMARRAP: *What Did He Do?*

Listen. Then clap and practice.

A. What did he   do?

B. He did   his homework.

A. What did she   sing?

B. She sang   a song.

A. What did they   hide?

B. They hid   their money.

A. Where did you   go?

B. I went to   Hong Kong.

A. What did he   lose?

B. He lost his   watch.

A. What did he   study?

B. He studied   French.

A. What did it   cost?

B. It cost   a lot.

A. What did they   buy?

B. They bought   a wrench.

K GRAMMARRAP: *I Was Talking to Bob When I Ran Into Sue*

Listen. Then clap and practice.

I was talking to   Bob when   I ran into   Sue.

I was waiting for   Jack when   I saw   Mary Lou.

They were cleaning   the house when   I knocked on the door.

He was dusting   a lamp when   it fell   on the floor.

She was learning to   drive when   I met her   last May.

She was buying   a car when   I saw her   today.

Activity Workbook   **19**

L WHAT'S THE QUESTION?

How	What	Where
How long	What kind of	Who
How many	When	Why

1. _____Who did you meet?_____   I met the president.

2. _____   She lost her purse.

3. _____   We did our exercises at the beach.

4. _____   They left at 9:15.

5. _____   She got here by plane.

6. _____   He sang in a concert hall.

7. _____   They stayed for a week.

8. _____   I saw a science fiction movie.

9. _____   He cried because the movie was sad.

10. _____   She wrote a letter to her brother.

11. _____   They complained about the telephone bill.

12. _____   We ate a lot of grapes.

13. _____   He spoke at the meeting.

14. _____   They lifted weights all morning.

15. _____   She gave a present to her cousin.

16. _____   I ordered apple pie.

17. _____   We rented seven movies.

18. _____   They sent an e-mail to their teacher.

19. _____   He fell asleep during the lecture.

20. _____   I lost my hat while I was skiing.

M OUR VACATION

1. A. Did you go to Hong Kong?

   B. No, _____we didn't_____.

   A. Where _____did you go_____?

   B. _____We went_____ to Tokyo.

3. A. Did your flight to Japan leave on time?

   B. No, _____.

   A. How late _____

   _____?

   B. _____ two hours late.

5. A. Did you stay in a big hotel?

   B. No, _____.

   A. What kind of _____

   _____?

   B. _____.

2. A. Did you get there by boat?

   B. No, _____.

   A. How _____?

   B. _____.

4. A. Did you have good weather during the flight?

   B. No, _____.

   A. What kind of _____

   _____?

   B. _____ terrible weather.

6. A. Did you eat American food?

   B. No, _____.

   A. What kind of _____

   _____?

   B. _____.

(continued)

7. A. Did you take your camera with you?

   B. No, _____.

   A. What _____

   _____?

   B. _____ our camcorder.

8. A. Did you get around the city by train?

   B. No, _____.

   A. How _____

   _____?

   B. _____.

9. A. Did you meet many Japanese?

   B. No, _____.

   A. Who _____?

   B. _____ other tourists.

10. A. Did you buy any clothing?

    B. No, _____.

    A. What _____?

    B. _____ souvenirs.

11. A. Did you speak Japanese?

    B. No, _____.

    A. What language _____

    _____?

    B. _____.

Where's the train station?

12. A. Did you spend a lot of money?

    B. Yes, _____.

    A. How much _____

    _____?

    B. ....

SOUND IT OUT! 🔊

Listen to each word and then say it.

this

1. chicken   3. river   5. busy

2. middle   4. kid   6. didn't

these

1. cheese   3. asleep   5. Steve

2. meat   4. receive   6. repeat

Listen and put a circle around the word that has the same sound.

1. clean: fine   middle   (these)

2. mix: ski   did   need

3. easy: Rita   break   eyes

4. video: machine   big   keep

5. east: build   little   green

6. symphony: mittens   life   retire

7. rip: knee   maybe   knit

Now make a sentence using all the words you circled, and read the sentence aloud.

8. ....

....

9. meat: Greek   Internet   eight

10. spill: healthy   his   rainy

11. promise: child   key   Richard

12. tea: every   men   into

13. cookie: with   speaks   bricks

14. milk: mine   advice   with

15. team: is   week   attractive

16. typical: sister   lazy   rebuild

Now make a sentence using all the words you circled, and read the sentence aloud.

17. ....

....

A. WHAT ARE THEY SAYING?

1. A. Did you ride your bicycle to work this morning?

   B. ___No, I didn't___ . I ___rode___ my

   motorcycle. ___I'm going to ride___ my bicycle to work tomorrow morning.

2. A. Did Tommy wear his new shoes to school today?

   B. _____. He _____

   his old shoes. _____ his new shoes tomorrow.

3. A. Did Sally give her husband a sweater for his birthday this year?

   B. _____. She _____

   him a tie. _____ him a sweater next year.

4. A. Did your parents drive to the mountains last weekend?

   B. _____. They _____ to

   the beach. _____ to the mountains next weekend.

5. A. Did you and your family have eggs for breakfast this morning?

   B. _____. We _____

   pancakes. _____ eggs tomorrow morning.

6. A. Did you go out with Mandy last Saturday night?

   B. _____. I _____

   out with Sandy. _____ out with Mandy next Saturday night.

7. A. Did Howard write an interesting story for homework today?

   B. _____. He _____ a

   boring one. _____ a more interesting story next time.

8. A. Did Shirley leave the office early this afternoon?

   B. _____. She _____

   very late. _____ early tomorrow afternoon.

BAD CONNECTIONS!

1. I'm really scared. Tomorrow my dentist is going to ##########.

   I'm sorry. I can't hear you. I think we have a bad connection. What's

   your dentist going to do ?

2. We're very excited about our trip. We're going to go to ###########.

   What did you say? I can't hear you. Where _____ _____?

3. My son is very sad. His girlfriend is going to move to Alaska because ############.

   I'm sorry. We have a bad connection. Why _____ _____?

4. My parents are going to give me a ########### for my sixteenth birthday.

   Excuse me. I can't hear you. _____ _____?

5. I'm really nervous. I'm going to ########### for the first time tomorrow.

   We have a bad connection. _____ _____?

6. Please come to our wedding. We're going to get married next ###########.

   I'm sorry. I can't hear you. _____ _____?

7. I won't be home after school today. I'm going to meet ############.

   This is a terrible connection! _____ _____?

(continued)

Listen and choose the time of the action.

1. a. last night
    b. tomorrow night

2. a. yesterday afternoon
    b. tomorrow afternoon

3. a. this weekend
    b. last weekend

4. a. this Saturday
    b. last Saturday

5. a. last week
    b. next week

6. a. yesterday evening
    b. this evening

7. a. tomorrow night
    b. last night

8. a. this weekend
    b. last weekend

9. a. this evening
    b. yesterday evening

10. a. last winter
     b. this winter

11. a. tomorrow morning
     b. yesterday morning

12. a. next semester
     b. last semester

James is a pessimist. He always thinks the worst will happen.

All his friends are optimists. They always tell James he shouldn't worry.

1. I'm afraid I ____won't have____ a good time at the office party tomorrow.

   Yes, ____you will____. ____You'll____ have a wonderful time.

2. I'm sure my son ____will hurt____ himself in his soccer match today.

   No, ____he won't____. ____He won't____ hurt himself. He's always very careful.

3. I'm afraid my grandmother _____ get out of the hospital soon.

   Yes, _____. _____ get out of the hospital in a few days.

4. I'm afraid my wife _____ upset if I get a very short haircut.

   No, _____. _____ be upset.

5. I'm positive I _____ weight on my new diet.

   Yes, _____. _____ lose a lot of weight.

6. I'm afraid my children _____ my birthday this year.

   No, _____. _____ forget your birthday. They never forget it.

7. I'm afraid my landlord _____ our broken doorbell.

   Yes, _____. _____ fix it as soon as he can.

8. I'm afraid my new neighbors _____ like me.

   Of course _____. _____ you a lot. Everybody likes you.

9. I'm sure _____ catch a cold when we go camping this weekend.

   No, _____. _____ catch a cold, James. You worry too much!

attend	browse	clean	do	fill out	rain	watch	work out

1. A. Will Amanda be busy this afternoon?

   B. Yes, _____she will_____ .

   _____She'll be doing_____ research at the library.

2. A. Will you be busy this evening?

   B. Yes, _____. _____

   _____ my income tax form.

3. A. Will Donald be home this afternoon?

   B. No, _____. _____

   _____ at his health club.

4. A. Will Mr. and Mrs. Lee be busy tonight?

   B. Yes, _____. _____

   _____ their apartment.

5. A. Will Grandpa be busy tonight?

   B. Yes, _____. _____

   _____ the web until after midnight.

6. A. Will you and your wife be home today?

   B. Yes, _____. _____

   _____ our favorite game show on TV.

7. A. Will Mom be home early tonight?

   B. No, _____. _____

   _____ a meeting.

8. A. Will the weather be nice this weekend?

   B. No, _____. _____

   _____ cats and dogs!

F A TOUR OF MY CITY

Pretend you're taking people on a tour of your city or town. Fill in the blanks with real places you know.

Good morning, everybody. This is .... speaking. I'm

so glad you'll be coming with me today on a tour of ....

We'll be leaving in just a few minutes.

First, I'll be taking you to see my favorite places in the city: ....,

...., and ....

Then we'll be going to .... for lunch. In my opinion, this is

the best restaurant in town. After that, I'll be taking you to see the other interesting

tourist sights: ...., ...,

and .... This evening we'll be going to ....

.... I'm sure you'll have a wonderful time.

G WHAT ARE THEY SAYING?

1. A. I'm sorry. I can't talk right now. I'm

    ____giving____ the kids a bath.

    B. How much longer _will you be giving_
    them a bath?

2. A. How much longer _____

    _____ your homework?

    B. I'll probably _____
    my homework for another half hour.

    A. Okay. I'll call you then.

3. A. Hi, Carol. This is Bob. Can you

    _____ for a minute?

    B. Sorry. I can't _____ right now.

    I'm _____ for a big test.

4. A. Sorry, Alan. I can't talk now. I'm

    _____ dinner with my family.

    B. How much longer _____

    _____ dinner?

Listen. Then clap and practice.

A.   Will you   be home   at a quarter   to three?
B.   Yes,   I will.   I'll be watching   TV.

A.   Will John   be home   at half   past two?
B.   Yes,   he will.   He'll be cooking   some stew.

A.   Will your parents   be home   today   at four?
B.   Yes,   they will.   They'll be washing   the floor.

A.   Will Jane   be home   if I call   at one?
B.   Yes,   she will.   She'll be feeding   her son.

A.   Will you   be home   at half   past eight?
B.   No,   I won't.   I'll be working   late.

A.   Will John   be home   at a quarter   to ten?
B.   No,   he won't.   He'll be visiting   a friend.

A.   Will your parents   be home   tonight   at nine?
B.   No,   they won't. They'll be standing   in line.

A.   Will Jane   be home   if I call her   at seven?
B.   No,   she won't.   She'll be dancing   with Kevin.

I WHOSE IS IT?

mine	his	hers	ours	yours	theirs

A. Hi, Robert. I found this wallet in my office today. Is it _____yours_____[1]?

B. No, it isn't _____[2], but it might be Tom's.

A. Maybe, but Tom hardly ever visits my office. It probably isn't _____[3].

B. It's small and blue. Maybe it's Martha's.

A. I asked her this morning. She says it isn't _____[4].

B. Is there anything inside the wallet?

A. There isn't any money, but there's a picture of three children.

B. It might belong to Mr. Hill. He and his wife have three children.

Maybe the children are _____[5].

A. I showed the picture to Mr. and Mrs. Hill. They said, "These

children aren't _____[6]. Our children are older."

B. Maybe you should give the wallet to our supervisor.

A. You know, it might be _____[7]. She has three children!

B. You're right. I'm positive it's _____[8]. I saw her children in her office last week.

J GrammarRap: *Where's My Coat?*

Listen. Then clap and practice.

A. Where's   my coat?   I can't find   mine.
   Is this one   mine   or yours?

B. That one is   mine.   It isn't   yours.
   Yours   is next to those doors.

A. Where's our umbrella?   We can't find   ours.
   Is this one   ours   or theirs?

B. That one is   theirs.   It isn't   yours.
   Yours   is under those chairs.

Circle the correct answer.

1. Jim is wearing a tuxedo today.
   a. He's going to visit his grandmother.
   b. He's going to a wedding.
   c. He's going to work in a factory.

2. My brother has a black eye.
   a. He painted his eye.
   b. He's wearing dark glasses.
   c. He hurt his eye.

3. The teacher wasn't on time.
   a. She was early.
   b. She was late.
   c. She didn't have a good time.

4. They chatted online yesterday.
   a. They used a cell phone.
   b. They used a computer.
   c. They used a fax machine.

5. Everyone in my family is going to relax this weekend.
   a. We're going to rest this weekend.
   b. We're going to retire this weekend.
   c. We're going to return this weekend.

6. He wasn't prepared for his exam.
   a. He didn't study for the exam.
   b. He didn't take the exam.
   c. He was ready for the exam.

7. Could I ask you a favor?
   a. I want to help you.
   b. I want to give you something.
   c. I need your help.

8. It's a very emotional day for Janet.
   a. She's going to work.
   b. She's getting married.
   c. She's studying.

9. He's composing a symphony.
   a. He's writing a symphony.
   b. He's listening to a symphony.
   c. He's going to a concert.

10. George ripped his shirt.
    a. He has to wash his shirt.
    b. He has to iron his shirt.
    c. He has to sew his shirt.

11. Can I borrow your bicycle?
    a. I need your bicycle for a little while.
    b. I want to give you my bicycle.
    c. I want to buy your bicycle.

12. Every day I practice ballet.
    a. I sing every day.
    b. I play violin every day.
    c. I dance every day.

13. I'm going to lend my car to Bob today.
    a. Bob is going to drive my car.
    b. I'm going to drive Bob's car.
    c. Bob is going to give me his car.

14. Mr. and Mrs. Hansen love to talk about their grandchildren.
    a. They listen to them.
    b. They're very proud of them.
    c. They argue with them.

15. Rita did very well on her exam.
    a. She's happy.
    b. She's anxious.
    c. She's sad.

16. I'm going to repair my washing machine.
    a. I'm going to paint it.
    b. I'm going to fix it.
    c. I'm going to do laundry.

17. I need to assemble my new desk.
    a. Can I borrow your screwdriver?
    b. Can I borrow your ladder?
    c. Can I borrow your chair?

18. I sprained my ankle.
    a. I broke my ankle.
    b. I hurt my ankle.
    c. I poked my ankle.

19. I'm going to fill out my income tax form.
   a. I'm going to return it.
   b. I'm going to read it.
   c. I'm going to answer the questions on the form.

20. They're playing Scrabble.
   a. They're playing a game.
   b. They're playing a sport.
   c. They're playing an instrument.

21. Mr. Smith is complaining to his boss.
   a. He's talking about his boss, and he's upset.
   b. He's talking to his boss, and he's happy.
   c. He's talking to his boss, and he's upset.

22. I'm going to call my wife right away.
   a. I'm going to call her immediately.
   b. I'm going to call her in a few hours.
   c. I'm going to call her when I have time.

23. My sister is an excellent athlete.
   a. She's an active person.
   b. She plays sports very well.
   c. She likes to watch sports.

24. My mother is looking forward to her retirement.
   a. She's happy about her new job.
   b. She wants to buy new tires for her car.
   c. Soon she won't have to go to work every day.

L LISTENING: *Looking Forward*

Listen to each story. Then answer the questions.

What Are Mr. and Mrs. Miller Looking Forward to?

1. Mr. and Mrs. Miller ____ last week.
   a. moved
   b. relaxed
   c. flew to Los Angeles

2. Mr. and Mrs. Miller aren't going to ____ this weekend.
   a. repaint their living room
   b. assemble their computer
   c. relax in their yard

3. They're going to ____ next weekend.
   a. assemble their computer
   b. relax
   c. paint flowers

What's Jonathan Looking Forward to?

4. Jonathan isn't ____ today.
   a. sitting in his office
   b. thinking about his work
   c. thinking about next weekend

5. Next weekend he'll be ____.
   a. working
   b. cooking and cleaning
   c. getting married

6. On their trip to Hawaii, Jonathan and his wife won't be ____.
   a. swimming in the ocean
   b. paying bills
   c. eating in restaurants

What's Mrs. Grant Looking Forward to?

7. When she retires, Mrs. Grant will be ____.
   a. getting up early
   b. getting up late
   c. taking the bus to work

8. Mrs. Grant will ____ with her friends.
   a. go to museums
   b. work in her garden
   c. read books

9. She'll take her grandchildren to ____.
   a. the park and the beach
   b. the zoo and the beach
   c. the park and the zoo

A. Fill in the blanks.

Ex. Ann ____is____ a good skater, and

her children __skate__ well, too.

1. A. Mr. and Mrs. Lee _____ wonderful dancers.

   B. I agree with you. They _____ very well.

2. A. Roger _____ very carelessly.

   B. I know. He's a terrible driver.

3. A. We don't swim very well.

   B. I disagree. I think _____ excellent _____.

4. A. I type very well. I think _____ a very good _____.

5. A. We _____ good _____, but we like to ski anyway.

B. Fill in the blanks.

1. A. Did you speak to Mrs. Baxter yesterday?

   B. No, I _____. I _____ too busy. But I _____ to Mrs. Parker.

2. A. Did you buy juice when you were at the store?

   B. No, I _____. I forgot. But I _____ milk.

3. A. _____ they get up early this morning?

   B. No, they _____. They _____ up very late.

4. A. Did Mr. Wong teach biology last semester?

   B. No, he _____. He _____ astronomy because the astronomy teacher _____ sick all semester.

5. A. _____ you talk to Tom last night?

   B. No, I _____. I _____ to his wife. Tom _____ there when I called.

C. Write the questions.

Ex. We're arguing with <u>our landlord</u>.

_____ *Who are you arguing with?* _____

1. I'm writing about <u>my favorite movie</u>.

   _____

2. They're going to fix <u>their bookcase</u>.

   _____

3. He hiked <u>in the mountains</u>.

   _____

4. She'll be ready <u>in a few minutes</u>.

   _____

5. They arrived <u>by plane</u>.

   _____

6. We'll be staying until <u>Monday</u>.

   _____

7. She's going to hire <u>five</u> people.

   _____

D. Answer the questions.

Ex. What did your daughter do yesterday morning?

(do her homework) _____ She did her homework. _____

1. What's your sister doing today?

(adjust her satellite dish) _____

2. What does your brother do every evening?

(chat online) _____

3. What are you going to do next weekend?

(visit my mother-in-law) _____

4. What did Jack and Rick do yesterday afternoon?

(deliver groceries) _____

5. What was David doing when his children came home from school?

(bake a cake) _____

6. How will you get to work tomorrow?

(take the bus) _____

7. What will you and your husband be doing this evening?

(watch TV) _____

8. How did you cut your hand?

(chop carrots) _____

E. Listen to each question and then complete the answer.

Ex. Yes, _____ he does _____ .

1. Yes, _____ .   5. No, _____ .

2. No, _____ .   6. Yes, _____ .

3. Yes, _____ .   7. No, _____ .

4. Yes, _____ .   8. Yes, _____ .

Read the first article on student book page 33 and answer the questions.

SIDE by SIDE Gazette

STUDENT BOOK
PAGES 33–36

1. More than 145 million immigrants ____.
   a. live outside
   b. move to be with family members
   c. live in urban neighborhoods
   d. leave their countries

2. ____ are examples of natural disasters.
   a. Political problems
   b. Bad living conditions
   c. Floods and earthquakes
   d. Wars

3. The main idea of paragraph 1 is immigrants ____.
   a. are everywhere
   b. have economic problems
   c. have political problems
   d. move for many different reasons

4. According to paragraph 2, many immigrants move from ____.
   a. North Africa to Western Europe
   b. Asia to Africa
   c. Latin America to Asia
   d. Western Europe to Eastern Europe

5. ____ has a larger percentage of immigrants than New York.
   a. Los Angeles
   b. Saudi Arabia
   c. Athens
   d. Rome

6. In Saudi Arabia ____ is native born.
   a. 10% of the population
   b. 40% of the population
   c. 50% of the population
   d. 90% of the population

7. The author refers to Esquilino as a *historic* neighborhood because ____.
   a. it's an urban neighborhood
   b. it has many Chinese immigrants
   c. it has a long history
   d. it has many schools that teach history

8. According to this article, in New York ____.
   a. the schools teach 140 languages
   b. 40% of the people were born in a foreign country
   c. 50% of the children are foreign born
   d. there are fewer immigrants than in Los Angeles

9. According to this article, ____.
   a. most immigrants are from Asia
   b. most immigrants live far from the city
   c. immigration changes neighborhoods
   d. most immigrants in Los Angeles are children

10. Immigrants probably move to urban neighborhoods because ____.
    a. urban neighborhoods have many jobs
    b. urban neighborhoods are very clean
    c. urban neighborhoods are expensive
    d. urban neighborhoods are historic

B FACT FILE

Look at the Fact File on student book page 33 and answer the questions.

1. The United States has twenty-four million more immigrants than ____.
   a. Germany
   b. Saudi Arabia
   c. Australia
   d. Canada

2. Canada has 600,000 more immigrants than ____.
   a. Germany
   b. Australia
   c. Saudi Arabia
   d. France

C ELLIS ISLAND

Read the second article on student book page 33 and answer the questions.

1. Ellis Island was an immigration center for ____.
   a. 54 years   c. 92 years
   b. 62 years   d. 100 years

2. Immigrants who came to the United States in ____ stopped at Ellis Island.
   a. 1800   c. 1900
   b. 1850   d. 1955

3. You can infer that immigrants who came to Ellis Island arrived ____.
   a. by plane   c. by bus
   b. by boat   d. by train

4. There weren't many immigrants from ____ at Ellis Island.
   a. Italy   c. Australia
   b. Germany   d. Austria

5. In paragraph 1, a *harbor* refers to ____.
   a. a building
   b. a neighborhood
   c. the ocean
   d. part of a body of water where boats can land

6. At Ellis Island officials DIDN'T ____.
   a. give English examinations
   b. check immigrants' documents
   c. give medical examinations
   d. send some immigrants back to their countries

7. Officials at Ellis Island probably gave medical examinations because ____.
   a. they wanted to help immigrants
   b. they were looking for doctors
   c. they didn't have enough hospitals
   d. they wanted to keep unhealthy people out of the country

D INTERVIEW

Read the interview on student book page 34 and answer the questions.

1. Tran came to Australia because ____.
   a. he wanted to learn English
   b. his wife's family was there
   c. his wife and children were there
   d. his brother's family was there

2. You can infer that Melbourne is ____.
   a. a city in Australia
   b. the capital of Australia
   c. a neighborhood in Australia
   d. a rural area in Australia

3. You know from the interview that ____ in Vietnam.
   a. Tran worked seven days a week
   b. Tran taught mathematics
   c. Tran's brother owned a restaurant
   d. Tran's wife had a good job

4. You can conclude that Tran does not work as ____.
   a. a waiter
   b. an assembler
   c. a cashier
   d. a cook

5. You can infer that Tran is working in a restaurant because ____.
   a. his brother owns the restaurant
   b. he likes to cook
   c. he has experience
   d. he wants to go to college

6. In the last sentence, *grateful* means ____.
   a. excited
   b. sure
   c. thankful
   d. nervous

E   WE'VE GOT MAIL! What's the Word?

Choose the words that best complete each sentence.

1. My birthday _____ tomorrow.
   a. will
   b. going to
   c. is
   d. is going to

2. The library _____ at 9 A.M. tomorrow.
   a. opening
   b. open
   c. opened
   d. opens

3. Jared _____ his parents in Miami next month.
   a. going to visit
   b. is visiting
   c. will going to visit
   d. going visiting

4. _____ getting married next June.
   a. We
   b. We'll
   c. We're
   d. We're going

5. Al's Department Store _____ a sale next week.
   a. is having
   b. having
   c. have
   d. will be

6. The bus to Canton _____ at 2:30 P.M.
   a. leaving
   b. leaves
   c. goes to leave
   d. going to leave

7. They _____ to the movies next Saturday.
   a. don't be going
   b. won't going
   c. can't going
   d. aren't going

8. The concert _____ in ten minutes.
   a. will
   b. begins
   c. going
   d. going to

F   WE'VE GOT MAIL! What's the Sentence?

Choose the sentence that is correct and complete.

1. a. The train arrived at 3:00 tomorrow.
   b. The train arriving at 3:00 tomorrow.
   c. The train arrives at 3:00 tomorrow.
   d. The train is going arrive at 3:00 tomorrow.

2. a. I'm taking a vacation next June.
   b. I go to take a vacation next June.
   c. I took a vacation next June.
   d. I'll be going to take a vacation next June.

3. a. The play starting at 6:30.
   b. The play will going to start at 6:30.
   c. The play going to start at 6:30.
   d. The play starts at 6:30.

4. a. There be no school tomorrow.
   b. There's no school tomorrow.
   c. There's being no school tomorrow.
   d. There going to be no school tomorrow.

5. a. We doing homework tonight.
   b. We're going to homework tonight.
   c. We're doing homework tonight.
   d. We'll be going to do homework tonight.

6. a. I'm going to skiing this weekend.
   b. I go to skiing this weekend.
   c. I going skiing this weekend.
   d. I'm going skiing this weekend.

FUN WITH IDIOMS!

Choose the best response.

1. I'll give you a ring tomorrow.
   a. Thanks. You're very generous.
   b. No thanks. I already have one.
   c. Give it to me now!
   d. Good. I'll talk to you then.

2. It's raining cats and dogs!
   a. Did you close all the windows?
   b. I think I'll walk the dog.
   c. Call the landlord and complain.
   d. There are too many pets in this neighborhood.

3. This job is no picnic.
   a. I'm glad you like it.
   b. The food is terrible.
   c. After a while, it will get easier.
   d. Have another piece of cake.

4. I'm tied up right now.
   a. I have a lot of free time, too.
   b. You look great.
   c. Is this a good time to talk?
   d. Sorry. I'll call you back later.

5. What's cooking?
   a. Fine thanks. And you?
   b. Not much.
   c. Are you hungry?
   d. I need a few things at the supermarket.

6. That homework assignment was a piece of cake. Do you agree?
   a. Yes. I finished it in ten minutes.
   b. Yes. I couldn't understand it.
   c. I don't agree. It was very easy.
   d. Yes. I have a stomachache.

H **"CAN-DO" REVIEW**

Match the "can do" statement and the correct sentence.

_____ 1. I can tell about current activities.

_____ 2. I can tell about past activities.

_____ 3. I can tell about future plans.

_____ 4. I can ask about likes.

_____ 5. I can tell about my goals.

_____ 6. I can describe my feelings and emotions.

_____ 7. I can react to bad news.

_____ 8. I can tell about the time of an event.

_____ 9. I can tell about the duration of an event.

_____ 10. I can ask a favor.

a. I'm going to wear my new jacket tomorrow.

b. I want to be a famous actor.

c. I'll be doing homework for another hour.

d. That's a shame!

e. I'm watching the news.

f. The movie will begin in a few minutes.

g. Do you like to swim?

h. Could you do me a favor?

i. I cleaned my apartment yesterday.

j. I was happy.

1. I ride horses.

   ___I've ridden___ horses
   for many years.

2. I fly airplanes.

   _____ airplanes
   for several years.

3. I give injections at the
   hospital.

   _____ injections
   for many years.

4. I speak Italian.

   _____ it
   all my life.

5. I take photographs.

   _____ them
   for many years.

6. I do exercises every day.

   _____ them
   every day for many years.

7. I draw cartoons.

   _____ cartoons
   for several years.

8. I write for a newspaper.

   _____ for a
   newspaper for many years.

9. I drive carefully.

   _____ carefully
   all my life.

B **LISTENING**

Listen and choose the word you hear.

1. a. ridden
   b. written

2. a. taking
   b. taken

3. a. giving
   b. given

4. a. written
   b. driven

5. a. writing
   b. written

6. a. drawing
   b. doing

7. a. spoken
   b. speaking

8. a. done
   b. drawn

I'VE NEVER

be	fly	give	ride	sing	take
draw	get	go	see	swim	write

1. _____I've never flown_____ in a helicopter.

2. _____ a raise.

3. _____ in a limousine.

4. _____ a cartoon.

5. _____ a book.

6. _____ a trip to Hawaii.

7. _____ in a choir.

8. _____ in the Mediterranean.

9. _____ on television.

10. _____ on a cruise.

11. _____ a present to my teacher.

12. _____ a Broadway show.

D **LISTENING**

Is Speaker B answering *Yes* or *No*? Listen to each conversation and circle the correct answer.

1. (Yes) No   3. Yes No   5. Yes No   7. Yes No

2. Yes No   4. Yes No   6. Yes No   8. Yes No

WHAT ARE THEY SAYING?

fall	get	give	go	ride	wear

1. A. _____Have you ever gotten_____ stuck in bad traffic?

   B. Yes. As a matter of fact, _____I got_____ stuck in very bad traffic this morning.

2. A. _____ on a Ferris wheel?

   B. Yes, I have. _____ on a Ferris wheel last weekend.

3. A. _____ a tuxedo?

   B. Yes, I have. _____ a tuxedo to my sister's wedding.

4. A. _____ scuba diving?

   B. Yes, I have. _____ scuba diving last summer.

5. A. _____ blood?

   B. Yes, I have. _____ blood a few months ago.

6. A. _____ on the sidewalk?

   B. Yes. In fact, _____ on the sidewalk a few days ago.

F **GRAMMARRAP:** *Have You Ever?*

Listen. Then clap and practice.

A. Have you ever   seen   a rainbow?

   Have you ever   learned   to dance?

   Have you ever   flown   an airplane?

   Have you ever   gone   to France?

B. No, I've never   seen   a rainbow.

   I've never   learned   to dance.

   I've never   flown   an airplane.

   But I've often   gone   to France.

WHAT ARE THEY SAYING?

drive	eat	go	meet	see	speak	take	write

1. A. __Have__ your children __eaten__ breakfast yet?

   B. Yes, __they have__. __They ate__ breakfast a little while ago.

2. A. _____ George _____ his new car yet?

   B. Yes, _____. _____ it for the first time this morning.

3. A. _____ Gloria _____ to the post office yet?

   B. Yes, _____. _____ to the post office a little while ago.

4. A. _____ you and Jane _____ the new movie at the Westville Mall?

   B. Yes, _____. _____ it last Saturday night.

5. A. _____ the employees _____ inventory yet?

   B. Yes, _____. _____ inventory last weekend.

6. A. _____ you _____ to the landlord yet?

   B. Yes, _____. _____ to him this morning.

7. A. _____ I _____ a letter to the Carter Company yet?

   B. Yes, _____. _____ them a letter last week.

8. A. _____ you and your wife _____ your daughter's new boyfriend yet?

   B. Yes, _____. _____ him last Friday night.

1. Kenji and his girlfriend aren't going to eat at Burger Town today. __They've__ already

    ___eaten___ at Burger Town this week. ___They ate___ there on Monday.

2. My sister isn't going dancing tonight. _____ already _____ dancing this week.

    _____ dancing last night.

3. Timothy isn't going to wear his new jacket to work today. _____ already _____ it to

    work this week. _____ it yesterday.

4. My husband and I aren't going to do our laundry today. _____ already _____ our

    laundry this week. _____ it on Saturday.

5. Roger isn't going to give his girlfriend candy today. _____ already _____ her

    candy this week. _____ her candy yesterday morning.

6. I'm not going to see a movie today. _____ already _____ a movie this week.

    _____ a movie on Wednesday.

7. We aren't going to buy fruit at the supermarket today. _____ already _____

    fruit at the supermarket this week. _____ some fruit two days ago.

8. Susie isn't going to visit her grandparents today. _____ already _____

    them this week. _____ them yesterday.

9. David isn't going to take his children to the circus today. _____ already _____

    them to the circus this week. _____ them to the circus a few days ago.

WHAT'S THE WORD?

| go |
| went |
| gone |

1. We should ____go____ now.

2. They ____went____ home early today.

3. She's already ____gone____ home.

| see |
| saw |
| seen |

4. I've never _____ him.

5. I _____ her yesterday.

6. Do you _____ them often?

| eat |
| ate |
| eaten |

7. I _____ there this morning.

8. Has he ever _____ there?

9. Do you _____ there every day?

| write |
| wrote |
| written |

10. How often do you _____ to them?

11. She's already _____ her report.

12. He _____ her a very long letter.

| wear |
| wore |
| worn |

13. When will you _____ it?

14. He's never _____ it.

15. She _____ it today.

| speak |
| spoke |
| spoken |

16. Who _____ to you about it?

17. She can't _____ Chinese.

18. Have they _____ to you?

| drive |
| drove |
| driven |

19. They've never _____ there.

20. We never like to _____ there.

21. She _____ there today.

| do |
| did |
| done |

22. Did you _____ your homework?

23. We _____ that yesterday.

24. Have you ever _____ that?

WHAT ARE THEY SAYING?

1. A. Janet, you've got to do your homework.

    B. But, Mother, __I've__ already _____
        my homework today.

    A. Really? When?

    B. Don't you remember? _____ my
        homework this afternoon.

    A. Oh, that's right. Also, _____ you

        _____ a letter to Grandma yet?

    B. Yes, _____. I wrote to her yesterday.

2. A. Would you like to swim at the health club
        tonight?

    B. I don't think so. _____ already _____
        at the health club today.

    A. Really? When?

    B. _____ there this morning.

3. A. Are you going to take your vitamins?

    B. _____ already _____ them.

    A. Really? When?

    B. _____ them before breakfast.

        How about you? _____ you _____ yours?

    A. Yes, _____. I _____ mine when I got up.

4. A. I hope Jimmy gets a haircut soon.

    B. Don't worry, Mother. _____ already _____
        one.

    A. I'm glad to hear that. When?

    B. _____ a haircut yesterday.

    A. That's wonderful!

5. A. When are you and Fred going to eat at the new restaurant downtown?

B. _____ already _____ there.

A. Really? When?

B. _____ there last weekend.

A. How was the food?

B. It was terrible. It was the worst food we've ever _____!

6. A. When are you going to speak to the boss about a raise?

B. _____ already _____ to her.

A. Really? When?

B. _____ to her this morning.

A. What did she say?

B. She said, ".."

K GRAMMARRAP: *Have You Gone to the Bank?*

Listen. Then clap and practice.

A. Have you gone to the   bank?

B.   Yes,   I have.

    I went to the   bank   at noon.

A. Have they taken   a vacation?

B.   Yes,   they have.

    They took   a vacation   in June.

A. Has he written   the letters?

B.   Yes,   he has.

    He wrote   the letters   today.

A. Has she gotten   a raise?

B.   Yes,   she has.

    She got   a raise   last May.

Activity Workbook   **43**

buy	dance	fly	go	read	see	swim
clean	eat	give	make	ride	study	take

1. A. What's the matter, Susan? You aren't riding very well today.

   B. I know. _____I haven't ridden_____ in a long time.

2. A. I can't believe it! These cars are very expensive.

   B. Remember, we _____ a new car in a long time.

3. A. Are you nervous?

   B. Yes, I am. _____ in an airplane in a long time.

4. A. Are you excited about your vacation?

   B. Yes, I am. _____ a vacation in a long time.

5. A. You aren't swimming very well today.

   B. I know. _____ in a long time.

6. A. Buster is really hungry.

   B. I know. He _____ anything in a long time.

7. A. Susie's room is very dirty.

   B. I know. She _____ it in a long time.

8. A. I think Timmy watches too much TV.

   B. You're right. _____ a book in a long time.

9. A. Mom, who was the sixteenth president of the United States?

B. I'm not sure. _____ American history in a long time.

11. A. Are you nervous?

B. Yes, I am. _____ blood in a long time.

13. A. Is there any fruit in the refrigerator?

B. No, there isn't. I _____ to the supermarket in a long time.

10. A. Everyone says the new movie at the Center Cinema is excellent.

B. Let's see it. We _____ a good movie in a long time.

12. A. What's Dad doing?

B. He's making dinner. _____ dinner in a long time.

14. A. Ouch!!

B. Sorry. _____ in a long time.

M PUZZLE: *What Have They Already Done?*

Across
1. wash
5. fly
8. go
10. explain
11. meet
12. take

Down
2. see
3. drive
4. play
6. wear
7. drink
8. get
9. be

Richard is going to have a party tonight, and he has a lot of things to do.

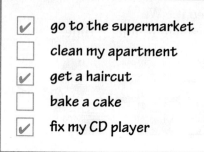

✔	go to the supermarket
☐	clean my apartment
✔	get a haircut
☐	bake a cake
✔	fix my CD player

1. _____ He's already gone to the supermarket. _____

2. _____ He hasn't cleaned his apartment yet. _____

3. _____

4. _____

5. _____

Susan is going to work this morning, and she has a lot of things to do.

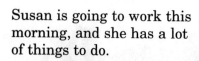

✔	take a shower
☐	do my exercises
☐	feed the cat
✔	walk the dog
☐	eat breakfast

6. _____

7. _____

8. _____

9. _____

10. _____

Beverly and Paul are going on a trip tomorrow, and they have a lot of things to do.

☐	do our laundry
✔	get our paychecks
✔	pay our bills
☐	pack our suitcases
☐	say good-bye to our friends

11. _____

12. _____

13. _____

14. _____

15. _____

Roberta is very busy today.
She has a lot of things to
do at the office.

☑	write to Mrs. Lane
☑	call Mr. Sanchez
☐	meet with Ms. Wong
☐	read my e-mail
☑	send a fax to the Ace Company

16. _____

17. _____

18. _____

19. _____

20. _____

You have a lot of things to do today. What have you done? What haven't you done?

1. ....

2. ....

3. ....

4. ....

5. ....

 **LISTENING** 🔊

What things have these people done? What haven't they done? Listen and check *Yes* or *No*.

		Yes	No			Yes	No
1.	do homework	✔	____	5.	do the laundry	____	____
	practice the violin	____	✔		vacuum the rugs	____	____
2.	write the report	____	____	6.	get the food	____	____
	send a fax	____	____		clean the house	____	____
3.	feed the dog	____	____	7.	speak to the landlord	____	____
	eat breakfast	____	____		call Ajax Electric	____	____
4.	fix the pipes	____	____	8.	hook up the VCR	____	____
	repair the washing machine	____	____		read the instructions	____	____

1. A. Have you spoken to David recently?

   B. Yes, I __have__. I _____ to him last night.

   A. What _____ he say?

   B. He's worried because he's going to fly in a helicopter this week, and he's never _____ in a helicopter before.

2. A. _____ you seen any good movies recently?

   B. No, I _____. I _____ a movie last week, but it was terrible.

   A. Really? What movie did you _____?

   B. *The Man from Madagascar.* It's one of the worst movies I've ever _____.

3. A. I think I forgot to do something, but I can't remember what I forgot to do.

   B. Have you _____ the mail to the post office?

   A. Yes. I _____ it to the post office an hour ago.

   B. _____ you _____ a fax to the Ace Company?

   A. Yes. I _____ them a fax this morning.

   B. _____ you _____ the employees their paychecks?

   A. Uh-oh! That's what I forgot to do!

4. A. _____ you gone on vacation yet?

   B. Yes, I _____. I _____ to Venice. It was phenomenal!

   A. _____ you ever _____ to Venice before?

   B. Yes, I _____. I _____ there a few years ago.

5. A. What _____ you get for your birthday?

    B. My family _____ me seventy-five dollars.

    A. That's fantastic! What _____?

    B. Going to buy? I've already _____ all my birthday money.

    A. Really? What _____ buy?

    B. I _____ a lot of songs. Do you want to _____ to them?

6. A. Are you ready to leave soon?

    B. No, _____. I haven't _____ a shower yet.

    A. But you _____ up an hour ago. You're really slow today. _____ you eaten breakfast yet?

    B. Of course _____. I _____ a little while ago, and I've already _____ the dishes.

    A. Well, hurry up! It's 8:30. I don't want to be late.

Q LISTENING

Listen to each word and then say it.

j!

1. job
2. jacket
3. juice
4. jam
5. jog
6. pajamas
7. journalist
8. just
9. Jennifer

y!

10. you
11. yoga
12. yellow
13. yard
14. yesterday
15. young
16. yogurt
17. yet
18. New York

R JULIA'S BROKEN KEYBOARD

Julia's keyboard is broken. The j's and the y's don't always work.
Fill in the missing j's and y's and then read Julia's letters aloud.

1.

Judy,

Have you seen my blue and
_yellow _jacket at __our house?
I think I left it there __esterday
after the __azz concert. I've looked
everywhere, and I __ust can't find
it anywhere.

        __ulia

2.

Dear __ennifer,

We're sorry __ou haven't been able
to visit us this __ear. Do __ou think
__ou could come in __une or __uly?
We really en__oyed __our visit last
__ear. We really want to see __ou
again.

        __ulia

3.

__eff,

__ack and I have gone out __ogging,
but we'll be back in __ust a few
minutes. Make __ourself comfortable.
__ou can wait for us in the __ard. We
haven't eaten lunch __et. We'll have
some __ogurt and orange __uice when
we get back.

        __ulia

4.

Dear __ane,

We __ust received the beautiful
pa__amas __ou sent to __immy.
Thank __ou very much. __immy is
too __oung to write to __ou himself,
but he says "Thank __ou." He's
already worn the pa__amas, and
he's en__oying them a lot.

        __ulia

5.

Dear __anet,

__ack and I are coming to visit
__ou and __ohn in New __ork. We've
been to New __ork before, but we
haven't visited the Statue of Liberty
or the Empire State Building __et.
See __ou in __anuary or maybe in
__une.

        __ulia

6.

Dear __oe,

We got a letter from __ames last
week. He has en__oyed college a lot
this __ear. His favorite sub__ects
are German and __apanese. He's
looking for a __ob as a __ournalist
in __apan, but he hasn't found one
__et.

        __ulia

S IS OR HAS?

1. He's already eaten lunch.
   _____ is
   ___✔___ has

2. He's eating lunch.
   ___✔___ is
   _____ has

3. She's taking a bath.
   _____ is
   _____ has

4. She's taken a bath.
   _____ is
   _____ has

5. He's having a good time.
   _____ is
   _____ has

6. She's going to get up.
   _____ is
   _____ has

7. He's bought a lot of music recently.
   _____ is
   _____ has

8. It's snowing.
   _____ is
   _____ has

9. She's thirsty.
   _____ is
   _____ has

10. He's got to leave now.
    _____ is
    _____ has

11. Where's the nearest health club?
    _____ is
    _____ has

12. She's written the report.
    _____ is
    _____ has

13. He's taking a lot of photographs.
    _____ is
    _____ has

14. He's taken a few photographs.
    _____ is
    _____ has

15. He's spent all his money.
    _____ is
    _____ has

16. There's a library across the street.
    _____ is
    _____ has

17. She's gone kayaking.
    _____ is
    _____ has

18. It's very warm.
    _____ is
    _____ has

19. He's embarrassed.
    _____ is
    _____ has

20. This is the best book she's ever read.
    _____ is
    _____ has

for   since

1. How long have you had a headache?

   I've had a headache

   __since__ this morning.

2. How long have your parents been married?

   _____ a long time.

3. How long has your brother owned a motorcycle?

   _____ last summer.

4. How long has your sister been interested in astronomy?

   _____ several years.

5. How long have you had a cell phone?

   _____ last month.

6. How long have you and your husband known each other?

   _____ 1994.

7. How long have the Wilsons had a dog?

   _____ a few weeks.

8. How long have you had problems with your upstairs neighbor?

   _____ a year.

9. How long has your daughter been a computer programmer?

   _____ 2000.

10. How long has your son played in the school orchestra?

    _____ September.

11. How long have there been mice in your attic?

    _____ two months.

1. <u>How long has</u> your daughter <u>wanted to be an engineer</u>?

   She's wanted to be an engineer for a long time.

2. _____ James _____?

   He's owned his own house since 2001.

3. _____ your grandparents _____?

   They've been married for 50 years.

4. _____ you _____?

   I've been interested in photography since last year.

5. _____ Gregory _____?

   He's worn glasses since last spring.

6. _____ your cousins _____?

   They've known how to snowboard for a few years.

7. _____ your son _____?

   He's had a girlfriend for several months.

8. _____ there _____?

   There's been a pizza shop in town since last fall.

A. How long have you   known   Maria?

B. I've known her   since I was   two.

A. Have you met   her older   sister?

B. No, I haven't.   Have you?

A. How long   has your son   been in college?

B. He's been there   since early   September.

A. Does he like   all of his   courses?

B. I think so.   I can't   remember.

A. How long have   your friends   lived in London?

B. They've lived there since two thousand   one.

A. Have you visited them   since they   moved there?

B. Yes, I have.   It was fun.

A. How long has   your brother   been married?

B. He's been married   for seven   months.

A. Have you seen him   since   his wedding?

B. I've seen him   only   once.

SINCE WHEN?

1. ____I'm____ sick today.

   ____I've been sick____ since I got up this morning.

3. Roger _____ how to ski.

   _____ how to ski since he took lessons last winter.

5. _____ lost.

   _____ lost since we arrived here this morning.

7. _____ cold and cloudy.

   _____ cold and cloudy since we got here last weekend.

9. My boyfriend _____ bored.

   _____ bored since the concert began forty-five minutes ago.

2. Rita _____ a swollen knee.

   _____ a swollen knee since she played soccer last Saturday.

4. _____ nervous.

   _____ nervous since they got married a few hours ago.

6. I _____ a stiff neck.

   _____ a stiff neck since I went to a tennis match yesterday.

8. My daughter _____ the cello.

   _____ played the cello since she was six years old.

10. _____ afraid of dogs.

   _____ afraid of dogs since my neighbor's dog bit me last year.

Listen and choose the correct answer.

1. a. Bob is in the army.
   b. Bob is engaged. *(circled)*

2. a. Carol is in music school.
   b. Carol is a professional musician.

3. a. Michael has been home for a week.
   b. Michael hurt himself this week.

4. a. She hasn't started her new job.
   b. She gets up early every morning.

5. a. Richard is in college.
   b. Richard hasn't eaten in the cafeteria.

6. a. Nancy and Tom met five and a half years ago.
   b. Nancy and Tom met when they were five and a half years old.

7. a. They play soccer every weekend.
   b. They're eight years old.

8. a. Patty is a teenager.
   b. Patty has short hair.

9. a. Ron used to own his own business.
   b. Ron moved nine years ago.

10. a. She's interested in astronomy.
    b. She's eleven years old.

11. a. He's in high school.
    b. He isn't in high school now.

12. a. Alan has owned his house for fifteen years.
    b. Alan doesn't have problems with his house now.

F CROSSWORD

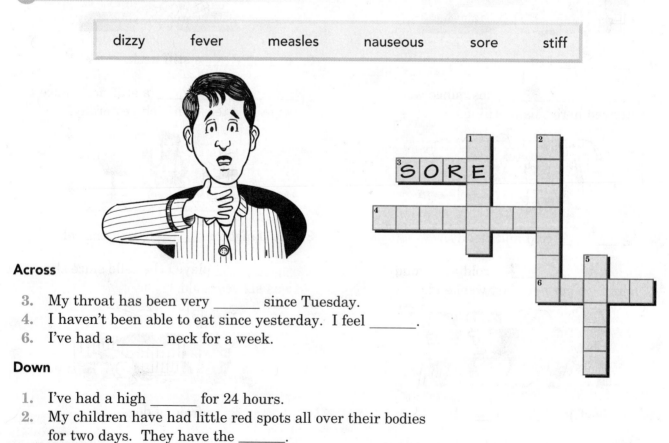

| dizzy | fever | measles | nauseous | sore | stiff |

Across

3. My throat has been very _____ since Tuesday.
4. I haven't been able to eat since yesterday. I feel _____.
6. I've had a _____ neck for a week.

Down

1. I've had a high _____ for 24 hours.
2. My children have had little red spots all over their bodies for two days. They have the _____.
5. I've been _____ since I fell down and hurt my head.

G SCRAMBLED SENTENCES

Unscramble the sentences.

1. she   a   jazz   Julie   liked   teenager.   has   was   since

   Julie has liked jazz since she was a teenager.

2. he   play   little   the   since   known   a   boy.   He's   piano   was   how   to

   _____

3. since   I've   was   in   I   astronomy   young.   interested   been

   _____

4. since   been   they   college.   engaged   They've   finished

   _____

5. been   he   a   cooking   He's   graduated   from   chef   school.   since

   _____

6. she   wanted   be   to   teacher   eighteen   She's   a   years   since   old.   was

   _____

7. moved   ago.   business   They've   their   year   owned   since   a   they   here   own

   _____

H WRITE ABOUT YOURSELF

1. I'm interested in ....

   I've been interested in .... since ....

2. I own ....

   I've owned .... since ....

3. I like ....

   I've .... since ....

4. I want to ....

   I've .... since ....

5. I know how to ....

   I've .... since ....

be	have	speak	teach	visit	walk

1. Mr. and Mrs. Miller __walk__ every day.

   _____ every day since Mr. Miller had problems with his heart last year. Before that, _____ never _____. They stayed home and watched TV.

2. Sam _____ with a Boston accent.

   _____ with a Boston accent since he moved to Boston last summer.

   Before that, _____ with a New York accent.

3. Terry _____ a truck driver. She drives a truck between the east coast

   and the west coast. _____ a truck driver for a year. Before that,

   _____ a taxi driver.

4. Before he moved to Brazil, Professor Baker

   _____ French. Now _____

   English. _____ English at a Brazilian university for the past two years.

5. Your Uncle Walter _____ already

   _____ us five times this year!

   Last year, he _____ us only twice. How many times will he

   _____ us next year?!

6. Tiffany _____ long blond hair.

   _____ long blond hair since she became a movie star. Before that, she

   _____ short brown hair. Tiffany looks very different now!

LOOKING BACK

Victor
(be)

musician	1990–now
photographer	1982–1989

Mrs. Sanchez
(teach)

science	1995–now
math	1985–1994

my grandparents
(have)

dog	1998–now
cat	1986–1997

Betty
(work)

bank	2000–now
mall	1997–1999

my parents
(live)

Miami	2001–now
New York	1980–2000

1. How long _____has Victor been_____ a musician?

   _____He's been a musician_____ since ___1990___ .

2. How long _____was he_____ a photographer?

   _____He was a photographer_____ for ___7 years___ .

3. How long _____ science?

   _____ since _____ .

4. How long _____ math?

   _____ for _____ .

5. How long _____ a cat?

   _____ for _____ .

6. How long _____ a dog?

   _____ since _____ .

7. How long _____ at the bank?

   _____ since _____ .

8. How long _____ at the mall?

   _____ for _____ .

9. How long _____ in New York?

   _____ for _____ .

10. How long _____ in Miami?

   _____ since _____ .

1. Do you still go skiing every winter?

No. ....
.... (for/since) ....
....

2. Do you still live ....
........................?

No. ....
.... (for/since) ....
....

3. Are you still a/an ....
........................?

No. ....
.... (for/since) ....
....

4. How long have you been interested in
........................?

....
.... (for/since) ....
....

5. Do you still ....
.... in your free time?

No. ....
.... (for/since) ....
....

6. Do your brothers still call you "Tiny Tim"?

No. .... (for/since) ....

7. How long have you .... ?

.... (for/since) ....

8. Do you still .... ?

No. .... (for/since) ....

L LISTENING

Listen and choose the correct answer.

1. a. He's always been a salesperson.
   b. He was a cashier. *(b is circled)*

2. a. His daughter was in medical school.
   b. His daughter is in medical school.

3. a. Her parents haven't always lived in a house.
   b. Her parents have always lived in a house.

4. a. He's always wanted to be an actor.
   b. He isn't in college now.

5. a. They exercise at their health club every day.
   b. They haven't exercised at their health club since last year.

6. a. James hasn't always been a bachelor.
   b. James has been married for ten years.

7. a. Jane has wanted to meet a writer.
   b. Jane wants to be a writer.

8. a. He's never broken his ankle.
   b. He's never sprained his ankle.

9. a. She's always liked rock music.
   b. She hasn't always liked classical music.

10. a. Billy has had a fever for two days.
    b. Billy has had a sore throat for two days.

11. a. Jennifer has always been the manager.
    b. Jennifer hasn't been a salesperson since last fall.

12. a. He's interested in modern art now.
    b. He's always been interested in art.

Read the article on student book page 65 and answer the questions.

1. A "24/7" company is open _____.
   a. 365 days a year
   b. 24 days a month
   c. 7 hours a day
   d. 24 weeks a year

2. The _____ is NOT an example of instant communication.
   a. telephone   c. mail
   b. fax   d. Internet

3. About 80% of all employees work _____.
   a. from 3:00 P.M. to 11:00 P.M.
   b. from 9:00 A.M. to 5:00 P.M.
   c. from 11:00 P.M. to 7:00 A.M.
   d. from 5:00 P.M. to 9:00 A.M.

4. International companies operate 24 hours a day because _____.
   a. they take care of emergencies
   b. many people like to work at night
   c. their employees need the money
   d. they have customers in different time zones

5. Until recently _____ have had a traditional daytime schedule.
   a. factory workers
   b. office workers
   c. firefighters
   d. nurses

6. When a local laundromat stays open 24 hours a day, it's probably because _____.
   a. its customers work different shifts
   b. its customers use the Internet
   c. it's an international company
   d. it sells products worldwide

7. According to this article, an employee of a "24/7" company _____.
   a. has to travel to other countries
   b. has to work 24 hours a day
   c. might have to work at night
   d. has to work overtime

8. The main idea of this article is _____.
   a. most businesses are open all day
   b. people work harder than they used to
   c. technology is creating more jobs
   d. technology is changing employees' work schedules

9. Which of these details DOES NOT support the main idea of the article?
   a. Many companies sell products worldwide.
   b. Local businesses have adjusted their hours.
   c. Some employees have switched to other shifts.
   d. Doctors and nurses work at night.

10. The purpose of this article is _____.
    a. to recommend types of jobs
    b. to describe changes in when people work
    c. to help night shift workers
    d. to complain about technology

B FACT FILE

Look at the Fact File on student book page 67 and answer the questions.

1. In _____ of the six countries, workers typically receive less than a month of vacation time.
   a. two
   b. three
   c. four
   d. five

2. A typical employee in Australia has _____ vacation time as a typical employee in the United States.
   a. the same amount of
   b. twice as much
   c. three times as much
   d. four times as much

C INTERVIEW

Read the interview on student book page 66 and answer the questions.

1. Mr. Souza gets to work at _____.
   a. 5:30 A.M.
   b. 6:30 A.M.
   c. 7:00 A.M.
   d. 3:00 P.M.

2. At 2:30 P.M., the children are _____.
   a. with their grandmother
   b. with their mother
   c. with their father
   d. at daycare

3. Mrs. Souza DOESN'T _____.
   a. do housework
   b. eat dinner with her children
   c. take the children to her mother's
   d. eat breakfast with her children

4. When Mr. Souza leaves work, his wife is _____.
   a. getting up
   b. doing housework
   c. starting work
   d. picking up the children

5. Mr. and Mrs. Souza spend time together _____.
   a. in the morning
   b. in the afternoon
   c. in the evening
   d. on the weekend

6. Mr. and Mrs. Souza can't communicate easily with each other because _____.
   a. they have too much housework
   b. their work schedules are different
   c. they don't write messages
   d. they don't have a telephone

7. Mr. Souza is probably asleep by 10:00 P.M. because _____.
   a. he doesn't have anything to do
   b. he lives on a quiet street
   c. he has to get up very early
   d. he doesn't want to wake up his wife

8. You can conclude that _____.
   a. the Souzas' children stay up late
   b. Mr. Souza likes his job
   c. Mrs. Souza is looking for a new job
   d. Mr. and Mrs. Souza work hard

D YOU'RE THE INTERVIEWER!

Interview a classmate, a neighbor, or a friend. Use the chart below to record the person's answers. Then share what you learned with the class.

Describe your typical day.	
When do you spend time with your family?	
What do you like about your schedule?	
What *don't* you like about your schedule?	

Choose the correct idiom to describe each person.

a couch potato	a real peach	chicken
a real ham	a smart cookie	the top banana

1. Roy is afraid to ask for a better work schedule. He's _____.

2. Lucy sits around and watches television all day. She's _____.

3. Edward is the funniest person I know. He's _____.

4. Miranda is the head of our company. She's _____.

5. Everyone loves Sally. She's _____.

6. Nancy knows more about computers than her teacher. She's _____.

F FUN WITH IDIOMS: Crossword

Across

4. A funny person is a
   _____.

6. A lazy person is a _____.

Down

1. A nice person is a _____.
2. An intelligent person is a
   _____.
3. A person who is afraid is
   _____.
5. The boss is the _____.

G FUN WITH IDIOMS: Writing

Do you know someone who is a ham? a real peach? a smart cookie? the top banana? Write about a person who "fits" one of these descriptions. Explain the reasons for your answer. Then share with your classmates.

H WE'VE GOT MAIL!

Choose the words that best complete each sentence.

1. I've already _____ dinner.
   a. eat   c. eaten
   b. eating   d. ate

2. He's never _____ a first-aid course.
   a. took   c. takes
   b. taking   d. taken

3. Randy hasn't _____ his homework yet.
   a. doing   c. did
   b. done   d. to do

4. She's _____ a teacher for a long time.
   a. was   c. already
   b. being   d. been

5. I've _____ to Chicago many times.
   a. driving   c. driven
   b. drove   d. went

6. _____ at this company since last year.
   a. I've worked   c. I worked
   b. I'm working   d. I work

Choose the sentence that is correct and complete.

7. a. I wasn't gone to the store yet.
   b. I haven't gone to the store yet.
   c. I haven't went to the store yet.
   d. I didn't gone to the store yet.

8. a. I've known Mary since I was young.
   b. I knew Mary since I've been young.
   c. I'm knowing Mary since I was young.
   d. I know Mary since I've been young.

9. a. I'm interested in art for many years.
   b. I'm being interested in art for many years.
   c. I've being interested in art for many years.
   d. I've been interested in art for many years.

10. a. We've already saw that play.
    b. We already seen that play.
    c. We've already seen that play.
    d. We're already seen that play.

11. a. They've never flown in an airplane.
    b. They've never flew in an airplane.
    c. They haven't never flown in an airplane.
    d. They never flown in an airplane.

12. a. She's speaking English for a year.
    b. She has spoken English for a year.
    c. She have spoken English for a year.
    d. She is spoken English for a year.

"CAN-DO" REVIEW

Match the "can do" statement and the correct sentence.

_____ 1. I can ask about a person's skills.

_____ 2. I can describe my work experience.

_____ 3. I can describe actions that have already occurred.

_____ 4. I can describe actions that haven't occurred yet.

_____ 5. I can ask about likes.

_____ 6. I can ask about a person's health.

_____ 7. I can describe an ailment or symptom.

_____ 8. I can tell about the duration of an illness.

_____ 9. I can react to information.

_____ 10. I can ask about the duration of an activity.

a. I haven't fed the dog yet.

b. I have a pain in my back.

c. How are you feeling?

d. I've written business reports for many years.

e. How long have you been interested in photography?

f. Do you like to swim?

g. Oh. I wasn't aware of that.

h. Do you know how to do yoga?

i. I've been sick for a week.

j. I've already gone to the supermarket today.

STUDENT BOOK
PAGES **69–80**

| for | since |

1. We've been living here __since__ 2001.

2. It's been raining _____ two days.

3. I've been listening to this music _____ an hour.

4. She's been flying airplanes _____ 1995.

5. Billy, you've been roller-blading _____ this morning!

6. He's been practicing the cello _____ three and a half hours.

7. Our neighbors have been vacuuming _____ 7 A.M.

8. We've been having problems with our heat _____ a week.

B CHOOSE

1. I've been working here since _____.
   a. last month
   b. three months

2. He's been taking a shower for _____.
   a. this afternoon
   b. half an hour

3. It's been ringing for _____.
   a. two o'clock
   b. a few minutes

4. She's been studying since _____.
   a. eight o'clock
   b. an hour

5. They've been dating for _____.
   a. high school
   b. six months

6. I've been feeling sick since _____.
   a. twelve hours
   b. yesterday

1. How long have you been studying?

   <u>I've been studying since</u>
   early this morning.

2. How long has Ann been feeling sick?

   _____
   a few days.

3. How long has Tom been having problems with his car?

   _____
   a week.

4. How long have the people next door been arguing?

   _____
   last night.

5. How long have we been waiting?

   _____
   forty-five minutes.

6. How long has that cell phone been ringing?

   _____
   the play began.

7. How long has Professor Drake been talking?

   _____
   an hour and a half.

8. How long have Rick and Sally been dating?

   _____
   high school.

9. How long have you been teaching?

   _____
   1975.

10. How long have I been chatting online?

    _____
    more than two hours.

WHAT ARE THEY DOING?

assemble	bake	bark	browse	do	jog	look	make	plant

1. Larry ____is looking____ for his keys.

   ____He's been looking____ for his keys all morning.

2. My sister _____ in the park.

   _____ in the park since 8 A.M.

3. The dog next door _____.

   _____ all day.

4. Our neighbors _____ flowers.

   _____ flowers for several hours.

5. Michael _____ his homework.

   _____ his homework since dinner.

6. My wife _____ the web.

   _____ the web for an hour.

7. Mr. and Mrs. Lee _____ their son's new bicycle.

   _____ it all afternoon.

8. I'm _____ cookies.

   _____ cookies since two o'clock.

9. You and your brother _____ a lot of noise!

   _____ noise since you got up.

E **LISTENING** 🔊

Listen and choose the correct time expressions to complete the sentences.

1. (a.) 1995.
   b. a few years.

2. a. 1:45.
   b. forty-five minutes.

3. a. 3 o'clock.
   b. thirty minutes.

4. a. yesterday.
   b. several days.

5. a. 7:30 this morning.
   b. more than an hour.

6. a. 7 o'clock.
   b. a half hour.

7. a. a few weeks.
   b. last month.

8. a. about three hours.
   b. 4 o'clock.

9. a. early this morning.
   b. twenty minutes.

Listen. Then clap and practice.

A.   How long have you been   working   at the mall?

B.   I've been working   at the mall   since the fall.

A.   How long has she been   wearing   her new ring?

B.   She's been wearing   her new ring   since the spring.

A.   How long have you been   living   in L.A.?

B.   We've been living   in L.A.   since May.

A.   How long has he been   waiting   for the train?

B.   He's been waiting   since it started   to rain.

A.   How long have you been   looking for   that mouse?

B.   We've been looking   since we rented   this house.

G WHAT ARE THEY SAYING?

make	play	run	snow	study	take	vacuum	wait	wear	work

1. Excuse me.

   Have you been waiting in line for a long time?

   Yes, I _have_.

   I've been waiting for more than an hour.

2. What a terrible day!

   _____ for a long time?

   Yes, _____.

   _____ since early this morning.

3. Your son plays the violin very beautifully.

   _____ lessons for a long time?

   Yes, _____.

   _____ lessons since he was five.

4. _____ here for a long time?

   No, _____.

   I've _____ here for only a week.

5. _____ your car _____ strange noises for a long time?

   Yes, _____.

   _____ these noises all week.

6. You look tired.

   _____ for a long time?

   Yes, _____.

   _____ all morning.

66 Activity Workbook

7. Your children speak French very well.

_____
it for a long time?

Yes, _____.

_____
French for six years.

8. I'm really tired.

_____
for a long time?

Yes, we _____.

_____
since 6 A.M.

9. Your pants are dirty.

_____
them all week?

No, _____.

_____
them for only a few hours.

10. This is the sixth game you've won today.

_____
for a long time?

No, _____.

_____
for only a few months.

H **LISTENING**

Listen and choose what the people are talking about.

1. (a.) traffic
   b. a computer

2. a. a wall
   b. the furniture

3. a. the guitar
   b. my bills

4. a. the drums
   b. tennis

5. a. the cookies
   b. the babies

6. a. the cake
   b. the bridge

7. a. her composition
   b. her bicycle

8. a. books
   b. trains

9. a. a sandwich
   b. a novel

10. a. socks
    b. chairs

11. a. the president
    b. songs

12. a. a restaurant
    b. a neighbor

13. a. fruit
    b. my car

14. a. a test
    b. a cake

15. a. videos
    b. problems

I SOUND IT OUT! 🔊

Listen to each word and then say it.

	th**i**s					th**e**se		

1. b**i**lls   3. ch**i**cken   5. b**ui**lding
2. off**i**cer   4. t**i**cket   6. **i**tself

1. w**ee**k   3. br**ie**fcase   5. f**e**ver
2. sp**ea**k   4. friendl**y**   6. **ea**ten

Listen and put a circle around the word that has the same sound.

1. th**i**n: pol**i**ce   t**i**red   (**i**nterested)
2. b**ui**ld: h**ea**dache   **i**s   sw**ea**ter
3. r**ea**d: St**e**ve's   b**ee**n   tr**y**
4. **i**f: **i**n   b**i**te   tax**i**
5. l**i**ve: m**e**t   h**i**story   ch**i**ld
6. f**i**shing: sc**i**ence   wr**i**ting   s**i**ster
7. p**ie**ce: ver**y**   w**ea**r   w**i**nter
8. **ea**st: h**i**re   Chin**e**se   r**ea**dy

Now make a sentence using all the words you circled, and read the sentence aloud.

9. ....

10. k**ey**:   d**i**nner   rec**ei**ve   th**i**nk
11. tenn**i**s: **ea**sy   h**ea**ter   th**i**s
12. compl**e**te: an**y**   g**e**t   tr**y**
13. k**ee**p: b**u**sy   P**e**ter   d**i**sturb
14. tux**e**do: t**y**pe   **i**f   w**ee**k
15. L**i**nda: d**i**dn't   gr**ee**n   br**i**ght
16. m**ee**ting: ch**i**ld   forg**e**t   **e**-mail

Now make a sentence using all the words you circled, and read the sentence aloud.

17. ....

J YOU DECIDE: *What Have They Been Doing?*

1. I have a sore throat.

No wonder you have a sore throat!

........*You've been singing*........ all day.

2. My back hurts.

No wonder your back hurts!

.... all day.

3. Bob has a terrible sunburn.

No wonder he has a terrible sunburn!

.... all day.

4. Nancy is very tired.

No wonder she's very tired!

.... all day.

5. Jane and I have headaches.

No wonder you have headaches!

.... all day.

6. Bob and Judy are very disappointed.

No wonder they're very disappointed!

.... all day.

7. I can't finish my dinner.

No wonder you can't finish your dinner!

.... all day.

8. Victor doesn't have any money.

No wonder he doesn't have any money!

.... all day.

| complain | eat | go | make | read | see | study | swim | talk | write |

1. My husband and I are very full. ___We've been eating___ for the past two hours. __We've__ already ____eaten____ soup, salad, chicken, and vegetables. And our dinner isn't finished. ___We haven't eaten___ our dessert yet!

2. Dr. Davis is tired. _____ patients since early this morning. _____ already _____ twenty patients, and it's only two o'clock. _____ the other patients in her waiting room yet.

3. Dave likes to swim. _____ for an hour and a half. _____ already _____ across the pool thirty times.

4. Amy is very tired. _____ to job interviews for the past three weeks. _____ already _____ to ten job interviews, and she hasn't found a job yet!

5. Gregory loves to talk. _____ all evening. _____ already _____ about his job, his house, and his car. Fortunately, _____ about his cats yet.

6. Betty and Bob are writing thank-you notes for their wedding gifts, and they're very tired. _____ them all weekend. _____ already _____ to their aunts, uncles, and cousins, but _____ to their friends yet.

7. Andrew is tired. He's having a party tonight, and _____ _____ desserts since early this morning. _____ already _____ two apple pies and three blueberry pies. But he isn't finished. _____ a chocolate cake yet.

8. Patty is very tired. _____ since she got home from school. _____ already _____ English and math. And she'll be up late tonight because _____ for her history test yet.

9. Today is Howard's day off, and he's enjoying himself. _____ _____ since early this morning. _____ already _____ three short stories. But _____ today's newspaper yet.

10. Mr. and Mrs. Grumble like to complain. _____ all evening. _____ already _____ about their jobs, the weather, and several members of their family. Fortunately, they _____ about the party yet, but I'm sure they will.

🔊 **LISTENING** 🔊

Listen and decide where the conversation is taking place.

1. (a.) in a kitchen
   b. in a supermarket

2. a. at home
   b. in school

3. a. in a department store
   b. in a laundromat

4. a. at a movie theater
   b. at home

5. a. at a clinic
   b. at a bakery

6. a. in a cafeteria
   b. in a library

7. a. at a concert hall
   b. at a museum

8. a. at a health club
   b. in a book store

9. a. in an office
   b. at a bus stop

10. a. at a zoo
    b. in a pet shop

11. a. at home
    b. at a movie theater

12. a. at a clinic
    b. in a department store

1. The floor is wet! How long has the ceiling been (leaking) / leaked ?

2. I'm not nervous. I've been flown / flying in helicopters for years.

3. I'm a little worried. I've never been running / run in a marathon before.

4. How many pizzas have you already made / been making so far today?

5. You look tired. What have you / have you been doing today?

6. I think I've seen / been seeing this movie before.

7. Has your husband already giving / given blood?

8. I've never taken / been taking a karate lesson. Have you?

9. Have you ever been going / gone out on a date before?

10. Alexander, your cell phone has rung / has been ringing since we started class!

11. Jane isn't nervous. She's been sung / singing in front of audiences for years.

N YOU DECIDE: *What Are They Saying?*

A. Mrs. Vickers, could I speak to you for a few minutes?

B. Of course. Please sit down.

A. Mrs. Vickers, I've been thinking. I've been working here at the

.... Company (for/since) ....
I've worked very hard, and I've done a lot of things here.

For example, I've .... ,

I've .... ,

and I've been ....

(for/since) ....

B. That's true, Mr. Mills. And we're happy with your work.

A. Thank you, Mrs. Vickers. As I was saying, I know I've done a
very good job here, and I really think I should get a raise.

I haven't had a raise (for/since) ....

B. ....

A. ....

A. Dad, could I speak to you for a few minutes?

B. Sure, James. Please sit down.

A. Dad, I've been thinking. I've been working very hard in school
this year, and I've done all my chores at home. For example,

I've .... , I've ....

.... , and I've been ....

.... (for/since) ....

B. That's true, James. Your mother and I are very proud of you.

A. Thank you, Dad. As I was saying, I know I've been very
responsible, and I really think I should be able to take your
car when I go out on a date. After all, I've been driving

(for/since) ....

B. ....

A. ....

Daniel has been living in a small town in Mexico all his life. His father just got a good job in the United States, and Daniel and his family are going to live there. Daniel's life is going to be very different in the United States.

1. He's going to live in a big city.
2. He's going to take English lessons.
3. He's going to take the subway.
4. He's going to shop in American supermarkets.
5. He's going to eat American food.
6. He's going to play American football.
7. He's going to ....

Daniel is a little nervous.

1. _____ He's never lived in a big city _____ before.

2. _____ before.

3. _____ before.

4. _____ before.

5. _____ before.

6. _____ before.

7. .... before.

Daniel's cousins have been living in the United States for many years. They'll be able to help him.

8. _____ They've been living in a big city _____ for years.

9. _____ for years.

10. _____ for years.

11. _____ for years.

12. _____ for years.

13. _____ for years.

14. .... for years.

Daniel's cousins tell him he shouldn't worry. They're sure he'll enjoy his new life in the United States very much.

YOU DECIDE: *A New Life*

.... has been living in ....

all her life. Now she's going to move to ....
(your city)

Her life is going to be very different in ....
(your city)

---

1. She's going to ....

2. She's going to ....

3. She's going to ....

4. She's going to ....

5. She's going to ....

_____ is a little nervous.

6. _____ before.

7. _____ before.

8. _____ before.

9. _____ before.

10. _____ before.

.... (has/have) been living in _____ for many
years and will be able to help her.

11. _____ for years.

12. _____ for years.

13. _____ for years.

14. _____ for years.

15. _____ for years.

_____ shouldn't worry. I'm sure she'll enjoy her new life in _____
very much.

✓ CHECK-UP TEST: Chapters 4–6

A. Complete the sentences with the present perfect.

Ex. *(do)*   Julie __has__ already __done__ her homework.

      (read)   I __haven't read__ your report yet.

(eat)   **1.** Mary and her brother _____ already _____ breakfast.

(take)   **2.** My nephew _____ his violin lesson yet.

(write)   **3.** I _____ to my grandparents yet.

(go)   **4.** My wife _____ already _____ to work.

(pay)   **5.** You _____ your electric bill yet.

(have)   **6.** Henry _____ already _____ a problem with his new cell phone.

B. Complete the questions.

1.   A. _____ to your supervisor yet?

     B. Yes, I have. I spoke to her this morning.

2.   A. _____ his new bicycle yet?

     B. Yes, he has. He rode it this morning.

3.   A. _____ their paychecks yet?

     B. Yes, they have. They got them this afternoon.

4.   A. _____ ever _____ in a helicopter?

     B. Yes, he has. He flew in a helicopter last summer.

5.   A. _____ ever _____ on TV?

     B. Yes, she has. She was on TV last week.

6.   A. _____ your daughter's new boyfriend yet?

     B. No, I haven't. I'm going to meet him tonight.

C. Complete the sentences.

Ex. My neck is very stiff. __It's been__ stiff since I got up this morning.

     Tom is reading his e-mail. __He's been reading__ it for a half hour.

1. It's sunny. _____ all week.

2. We're browsing the web. _____ the web since 8 o'clock.

3. My daughter has a fever. _____ a fever since early this morning.

4. My son is studying. _____ since he got home from school.

5. Our neighbors are arguing. _____ all afternoon.

6. I know how to skate. _____ how to skate since I was six years old.

7. Susan is interested in science. _____ interested in science since she was a teenager.

8. My husband and I are cleaning our basement. _____ it all weekend.

D. Complete the answers.

| for | since |

1. How long has your wife been working at the bank?

   _____ 1999.

2. How long have those dogs been barking?

   _____ a long time.

3. How long has it been snowing?

   _____ two days.

4. How long have you wanted to be an astronaut?

   _____ I was six years old.

E. Complete the sentences.

1. My brother owns a motorcycle. _____ a motorcycle since last summer.

   Before that, _____ a bicycle.

2. I'm a journalist. _____ a journalist since 2000.

   Before that, _____ an actor.

3. My daughter likes classical music. _____ classical music since she finished college.

   Before that, _____ rock music.

F. Listen and choose the correct answer.

1. a. Janet is in acting school.
   b. Janet is an actress.

2. a. The president has finished his speech.
   b. The president is still speaking.

3. a. They've been living in New York since 1995.
   b. They haven't lived in New York since 1995.

4. a. They're going to eat later.
   b. They're going to eat now.

5. a. She's called the superintendent.
   b. She has to call the superintendent.

6. a. Someone is helping Billy with his homework.
   b. No one is helping Billy with his homework.

A WHAT DO THEY { ENJOY DOING / LIKE TO DO } ?

| enjoy _____ing | like to _____ | _____ing |

1. My wife and I ____enjoy____ relaxing on the beach when we go on vacation.

2. Mrs. Finn is very talkative. She ____likes to____ talk about her grandchildren.

   ____Talking____ about her grandchildren is important to her.

3. Billy doesn't _____ going to the doctor, but he went yesterday for his annual checkup.

4. I _____ knit sweaters. _____ sweaters is a good way to relax.

5. My husband doesn't _____ asking for a raise, but sometimes he has to.

6. Dr. Brown _____ deliver babies. In her opinion, _____ babies is the best job in the world.

7. Bob doesn't _____ being a bachelor. He thinks _____ married is better.

8. Ann _____ plant flowers. She thinks _____ flowers is good exercise.

9. Jim _____ chatting online with his friends, but his parents think _____ online every evening isn't a very good idea.

10. Tom doesn't _____ play hockey. He thinks _____ hockey is dangerous.

11. My parents go to the gym during the winter, but in the summer they _____ going hiking.

12. Martin _____ go to parties. He thinks _____ to parties is a good way to meet people.

13. I really want to play the piano well, but I don't _____ practicing.

Listen. Then clap and practice.

Writing is   fun.

I like to   write.

I enjoy   writing letters   late   at night.

Eating is   fun.

I like to   eat.

I enjoy eating   fish,   and I like eating   meat.

Skiing is   great.

He likes to   ski.

But skiing's been   hard   since he hurt   his knee.

Singing is   fun.

She likes to   sing.

But today   she's sick,   and she can't sing   a thing.

Running is   great.

They like to   run.

Swimming's   okay,   but running's   more fun.

Baking is   great.

He likes to   bake.

When he's feeling   sad,   he bakes   a cake.

Knitting is   fun.

She likes to   knit.

She enjoys knitting   sweaters,   but none of them   fit!

WHAT'S THE WORD?

clean	complain	eat	go	sit	wear
cleaning	complaining	eating	going	sitting	wearing

1. I hate to ____*complain*____, but your loud music is disturbing me.

2. Carol tries to avoid _____ in the sun.

3. Sally likes to _____ dinner at home.

4. My son hates to _____ his room.

5. Richard can't stand to _____ a tie.

6. Tom avoids _____ his apartment whenever he can.

7. James doesn't like to _____ to the mall.

8. My husband and I hate _____ sailing.

9. My wife and I like to _____ in the park on a sunny day.

10. Please try to avoid _____ about the weather all the time.

11. My friends and I can't stand _____ in fast-food restaurants.

12. My daughter likes _____ the sweater you gave her for her birthday.

D **GRAMMARRAP:** *Pet Peeves*

Listen. Then clap and practice.

I don't like   waiting   for the bus   in the rain.

I hate to   rush   when I'm late   for a plane.

I avoid   talking   to strangers   on the train.

I can't stand   driving   in the center   lane.

I don't like to   iron   on a hot   summer day.

I hate to clean   the house   in the middle   of May.

I avoid   dusting   and sweeping   my floors.

I can't stand   doing   all my household   chores!

YOU DECIDE: *What's the Reason?*

1. David is happy he works in a gym because he enjoys

   exercising every day..

2. Gloria hates being a taxi driver because she can't stand

   ....

3. Miguel is glad he lives in Puerto Rico because he likes

   ....

4. I'm sorry I'm a secretary because I can't stand

   ....

5. We're happy we're going camping because we enjoy

   ....

6. William is upset he's sick because he hates

   ....

7. I'm glad I have a new bicycle because I like

   ....

8. Norman doesn't like being on a diet because he can't stand

   ....

9. Julie is happy she's a Hollywood actress because she enjoys

   ....

F MY ENERGETIC GRANDFATHER

A. Your grandfather is very energetic!

B. He sure is!

A. When did he start _____ [1] the drums?

B. Believe it or not, he learned _____ [2] the drums when he was sixty years old!

A. That's incredible! Does he _____ [3] the drums often?

B. Yes, he does. He's played every day for the last eight years.

A. What else does he enjoy doing?

B. He enjoys _____ [4], he enjoys _____ [5], and he also enjoys _____ [6].

A. I hope I have that much energy when I'm his age!

G I CAN'T STAND IT!

I spoke with my friend Pam last weekend, and she talked a lot about figure skating. Ever since she started to figure skate several months ago, that's all she ever talks about! I never go out with her anymore because she practices figure skating all the time. And whenever I talk to her on the phone, figure skating is the only thing she talks about! (She thinks that everybody should learn to figure skate.) I can't stand it! I don't ever want to hear another word about figure skating!

Now YOU tell about somebody.

I spoke to my friend .... last weekend, and .... talked a lot about

.... Ever since ....

....

....

....

....

....

H CHOOSE

1. I've decided ⟨buy / buying / (to buy)⟩ a motorcycle.

2. Have you ever considered ⟨to move / moving / move⟩ ?

3. I'm thinking about ⟨going / to go / go⟩ on a diet.

4. You should consider ⟨to change / change / changing⟩ jobs.

5. Have you decided to ⟨get / to get / getting⟩ a dog?

6. He's thought about ⟨to retire / retiring / retire⟩ .

I GRAMMARRAP: *I Considered Ordering the Cheesecake*

Listen. Then clap and practice.

I considered   ordering the cheesecake.
Everyone   said I should   try it.
But then   I decided   to skip   dessert.
I wanted to   stay   on my diet.

I thought about   going   home early.
It was only   a quarter to   ten.
But I changed   my mind and   decided to   stay
When the music   started   again.

I thought about   moving to   France
And studying   music and   dance.
But I changed   my mind and   decided to   stay
With my cat   and my bird and my   plants.

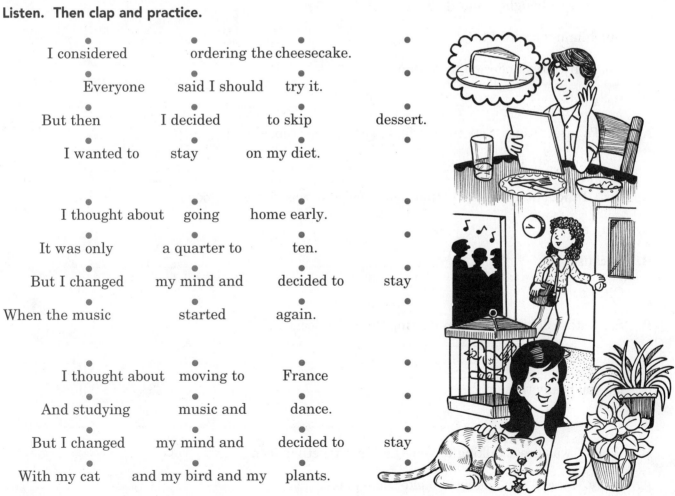

YOU DECIDE: *What's Carla Going to Do?*

A. Hi, Carla. How are you? We haven't spoken in a long time. Tell me, what have you been doing?

B. ....

A. Oh. And what are you thinking about doing after you finish studying English?

B. For a while, I considered ....,

and then I thought about ....

But I finally decided to ....

A. Oh. Why did you decide to do that?

B. Because ....

A. That's interesting. Tell me, Carla, have you ever considered ....

....?

B. Yes. I thought about doing that, but decided it wasn't a very good idea.

A. Why not?

B. Because ....

A. Oh, I see.

B. So, Kathy, do you think I'm making the right decision?

A. ....

B. Do you really think so?

A. ....

B. Well, it was great talking to you. Let's get together soon.

A. Okay. I'll call you and we'll make some plans.

1. You can't keep on ____rearranging____ the furniture so often. You rearranged it last weekend!

2. I stopped _____ meat. I only eat fish and chicken.

3. He tried to quit _____, but he couldn't. He still worries about everything.

4. Alice always gets up late. She should start _____ up earlier.

5. Richard doesn't exercise very often. He should begin _____ every day. He'll feel a lot better.

6. You can't continue _____ me the same question. You've already asked me ten times!

7. I realize that I can't keep on _____ with people. I'm never going to argue with anyone again!

8. I know that Dave takes piano lessons. When did he start _____ guitar lessons?

9. You should stop _____ your bills late and start _____ them on time.

10. Professor Blaine is very boring. Students continue _____ asleep in his classes.

L **GOOD DECISIONS**

bite	clean	cook	do	gossip	interrupt	make	pay

This year I'm going to break all my bad habits. First, I've decided to stop ___biting___ [1] my nails. I've also started _____ [2] exercises every day. I learned _____ [3] when I was young, so I've decided to start _____ [4] healthy meals. I'm also considering _____ [5] my bills on time, and I'm thinking about _____ [6] my apartment every week. I've also decided to stop _____ [7] about other people and to stop _____ [8] my friends while they're talking.

1. My husband can't stop ____falling____ asleep at the movies. Every

time we go, he falls asleep. If he keeps on _____ asleep,
I'll never go to a movie with him again.

2. I don't think I should continue _____ weights every day. I

like _____ weights, but I'm afraid I might hurt my back if I

keep on _____ them so often.

3. My older sister always teases me. Today I'm really mad! She began

_____ me early this morning, and she hasn't stopped. If

she keeps on _____ me, I'm going to cry. And I won't

stop _____ until she stops _____ me!

4. My friend Albert has got to stop _____ so fast and start

_____ more carefully. If he continues _____
fast, I'm sure he'll have a serious accident some day.

5. Mr. Perkins, when are you going to stop _____ so sloppily

and start _____ more neatly? If you keep on

_____ like that, I'm going to have to fire you.

6. My boyfriend is very clumsy. When we go dancing, he keeps on

_____ on my feet. If he doesn't start _____

more gracefully, I'm going to stop _____ dancing with him.

Listen and choose the correct answer.

1. a. delivering babies.
   b. fix broken legs.

2. a. eating junk food.
   b. to pay our bills late.

3. a. swimming.
   b. to play golf.

4. a. to tap dance.
   b. figure skating.

5. a. to work out at a health club every week.
   b. retiring.

6. a. taking karate lessons.
   b. mend my pants.

7. a. to go back to college?
   b. moving?

8. a. to argue with people.
   b. biting my nails.

9. a. teasing your sister?
   b. to go to bed so late?

10. a. eat fruits and vegetables.
    b. worrying about my health all the time.

11. a. stand in line.
    b. wearing a suit.

12. a. taking photographs?
    b. study the piano?

13. a. to do his homework.
    b. clean his apartment.

14. a. studying engineering.
    b. teach a computer course.

15. a. to live at home.
    b. going to school for the rest of your life.

O **WHAT DOES IT MEAN?**

Choose the correct answer.

1. My wife is very dizzy.
   a. I'm glad to hear that.
   b. How long has she been feeling sick?
   c. I guess she has a lot of things to do.

2. Peter and Nancy are vegetarians.
   a. They've quit eating vegetables.
   b. They've stopped planting flowers.
   c. They've stopped eating meat.

3. Andrew avoids talking about politics.
   a. He doesn't like talking about politics.
   b. He enjoys talking about politics.
   c. He's learning to talk about politics.

4. Shirley has worked her way to the top.
   a. She's the tallest person in her family.
   b. She's the president of her company.
   c. She works on the top floor of her building.

5. The people across the street were furious.
   a. They were embarrassed.
   b. They were awkward.
   c. They were very angry.

6. What's your present occupation?
   a. What do you do now?
   b. What are you going to do?
   c. What did you do when you were young?

7. This is my father-in-law, Mr. Kramer.
   a. He just graduated from high school.
   b. He just retired.
   c. He's seventeen years old.

8. My mother is going to mend my socks.
   a. She's going to fix them.
   b. She's going to wash them.
   c. She's going to send them to my sister.

9. You should stop gossiping.
   a. You should stop interrupting people.
   b. You should stop bumping into people.
   c. You should stop talking about people.

10. I've decided to ask for a raise.
    a. You should speak to your landlord.
    b. You should speak to your boss.
    c. You should speak to your instructor.

11. Dr. Wu has a lot of patients.
    a. That's true. She never gets angry.
    b. I know. She's a very popular doctor.
    c. That's true. She never gets sick.

12. My Uncle Gino has an Italian accent.
    a. He bought it when he went to Italy.
    b. He wears it all the time.
    c. Everybody knows he's from Italy.

1. Lisa didn't feel very well when she got up this morning because

   she *(eat)* __had__ __eaten__ a lot of candy before she went to bed.

2. My husband invited his boss for dinner last Friday night, and he forgot to tell me.

   Unfortunately, I *(get)* _____ already _____ tickets for a concert.

3. Our friends didn't stop showing us pictures of their grandson all evening. They

   (visit) _____ just _____ him the day before.

4. I wanted to drive to the mountains with my friends yesterday, but they *(drive)* _____

   _____ to the mountains the afternoon before.

5. Andrew wasn't very happy when I visited him yesterday. He *(cut)* _____ just _____
   himself while he was cooking dinner.

6. Alice couldn't buy the new printer she wanted because she *(spend)* _____ _____
   all her money on her vacation.

7. When my son got home from his date last night, my wife and I *(go)* _____ already

   _____ to sleep.

8. My children didn't want to eat pancakes for breakfast yesterday morning because

   I *(make)* _____ _____ pancakes the morning before.

9. I didn't see a movie with my friends last weekend because I *(see)* _____ _____
   three movies the weekend before.

10. When I got up this morning, my wife *(leave)* _____ already _____ for work.

11. Norman was upset when I saw him yesterday morning. He *(have)* _____ _____
    a big argument with his next-door neighbor the night before.

12. When I saw Jill today, she was very happy. Her boyfriend *(give)* _____ just _____
    her a beautiful bracelet for her birthday.

13. Tom couldn't lend me his dictionary the other day because he *(lose)* _____ _____
    it the week before.

Listen. Then clap and practice.

She felt very   happy   when she left   the store.
She had never   bought   a computer   before.

He looked   very nervous when he   knocked   on the door.
He had never   gone out   on a date   before.

She felt very   weak,   and her throat was   sore.
She had never   had   the flu   before.

He felt   very proud   when his guests asked for   more.
He had never   baked   a pie   before.

She felt   very foolish   when her food   hit the floor.
She had never   eaten   with chopsticks   before.

He looked   very scared   when it started to   roar.
He had never   been close   to a lion   before.

She was very   annoyed   when he started to   snore.
He had never   made   so much noise   before.

He was very   surprised   when he opened   the drawer.
He had never   seen   so much money   before.

Gary Gray was very upset yesterday. He didn't get up until 9:00, and as a result, he was late for everything all day!

Today's meeting begins at 10:00.

2. He drove to the office and arrived late for an important meeting.

It _____ already _____.

Bank Closes at 3:00.

4. He got to the bank at 3:15, but he was too late. It _____ already _____.

To: garyg@go.com
From: tom@hopmail.com

I'll be leaving at 4:30. Hope to see you before then.

6. He had made plans to get together with his friend Tom. But he didn't get to Tom's office until 5:00. His friend Tom

_____ already _____.

Last train to Centerville leaves at 9:30.

1. He got to the train station at 9:45. The train __had__ already ____left____.

To: garyg@go.com
From: janet@hopmail.com

Let's have lunch at 12:00. I have to go back to work at 12:45.

3. He got to the restaurant at 1:00 to meet his friend Janet for lunch. However, she _____ already _____ back to work.

Professor Tweedle's Lecture on Bird-Watching Starts at 4:00.

5. He got to the bird-watching lecture at 4:15. It _____ already _____.

Dear Gary,
    Our plane will be arriving at the airport at 8:10. We're looking forward to seeing you.
            Love,
            Grandma & Grandpa

7. He drove to the airport to pick up his grandmother and grandfather. He got to the airport at 8:30. Their plane

_____ already _____.

IN A LONG TIME

1. We got lost on the way to the party last night. We *(listen)* ___hadn't___ ___listened___ very carefully to the directions.

2. I enjoyed seeing my old friends at my high school reunion last weekend.

   I *(see)* _____ _____ them since we finished high school.

3. My wife and I decided to have a picnic in the park last Sunday. We *(have)* _____

   _____ a picnic in the park in a long time.

4. I went dancing with my girlfriend last Saturday night, and I hurt my back.

   I *(go)* _____ _____ dancing in a long time.

5. Cynthia was embarrassed at her party last night. She had invited her cousin Charles, but

   she *(remember)* _____ _____ to invite his girlfriend, Louise.

6. Frank looked terrible when I saw him yesterday. His pants were dirty, he

   (iron) _____ _____ his shirt, and he *(shave)* _____ _____
   in several days.

7. Michael was very discouraged when I saw him last week. He had been on a diet for a month,

   and he *(lose)* _____ _____ any weight.

8. Sylvia fell several times while she was skiing last weekend. She *(ski)* _____

   _____ in a long time.

9. Arnold's boss fired him last week. Arnold *(get)* _____ _____ to work on time
   in six months.

10. Betty was very lucky she didn't miss her plane this morning. She got to the airport late, but

    the plane *(take off)* _____ _____ yet.

11. Alan did poorly on his English exam last week. I'm not surprised. He *(study)* _____

    _____ for the test.

12. Stuart enjoyed riding his bicycle last weekend. He *(ride)* _____ _____ it in a
    long time.

Jennifer was very busy after school yesterday.

1:00	write an English composition
2:00	study for my science test
3:00	practice the trombone
4:00	read the next history chapter
5:00	memorize my lines for the school play

What was she doing at 2:00?

1. _____ She was studying for her science test. _____

What had she already done?

2. _____ She had already written an English composition. _____

What hadn't she done yet?

3. _____ She hadn't practiced the trombone yet. _____

4. _____

5. _____

Brian had a very busy day at the office yesterday.

9:00	send an e-mail to the boss
10:00	give the employees their paychecks
11:00	hook up the new printer
1:00	write to the Bentley Company
2:00	take two packages to the post office

What was he doing at 11:00?

6. _____

What had he already done?

7. _____

8. _____

What hadn't he done yet?

9. _____

10. _____

Mr. and Mrs. Mendoza had a very busy day at home yesterday.

8:00	assemble Billy's new bicycle
9:00	fix the fence
11:00	clean the garage
2:00	repair the roof
4:00	start to build a tree house

What were they doing at 11:00?

11. _____

What had they already done?

12. _____

13. _____

What hadn't they done yet?

14. _____

15. _____

Brenda wants to lose some weight, so she had a very busy day at her health club.

9:00	do yoga
10:00	go jogging
12:00	play squash
3:00	lift weights
4:00	swim across the pool 10 times

What was she doing at 12:00?

16. _____

What had she already done?

17. _____

18. _____

What hadn't she done yet?

19. _____

20. _____

WHAT HAD THEY BEEN DOING?

1. Professor Smith finally ended his lecture at 6:00. He *(talk)* _____ had been talking _____ for three hours.

2. The Millers moved out of their apartment building last week. They *(live)* _____

   _____ there for several years.

3. Our daughter lost her job last week. She *(work)* _____ at the same company since she graduated from college.

4. Peter was happy when he and his girlfriend finally got married. They *(go out)* _____

   _____ for eight years.

5. We were sad when Rudy's Restaurant closed. We *(plan)* _____ to eat there on our anniversary.

6. We felt very nostalgic when we went back to our hometown. We *(think about)* _____

   _____ going back there for a long time.

7. My husband and I were happy when our son decided to study harder. He *(get)* _____

   _____ poor grades in school.

8. Mr. Best was happy when his neighbor bought his own ladder. He *(borrow)* _____

   _____ Mr. Best's ladder for many years.

9. I'm not surprised that Lenny's doctor put him on a diet. Lenny *(eat)* _____
   too many fatty foods.

10. It's too bad your daughter wasn't able to perform in her violin recital last weekend. She

    (rehearse) _____ for it for a long time.

11. I'm sorry you had to cancel your trip to Hawaii. You and your wife *(look forward)* _____

    _____ to it for a long time.

12. I'm so happy that Sally won the marathon last weekend. She *(train)* _____
    for it for the past six months.

13. Nobody at the office was surprised when Mrs. Anderson fired Frank, her new assistant. He

    (arrive) _____ late for work every day for the past month.

G GRAMMARRAP: *George Had Been Thinking of Studying Greek*

Listen. Then clap and practice.

George had been thinking of studying Greek,
Moving to Athens and learning to speak.
But he changed his mind and decided to stay
With his family and friends and his dog in L.A.

Jill had been planning to learn how to ski,
But she tripped and fell and sprained her knee.
She had been dreaming of mountains and snow.
But now she's at home and has no place to go.

Marie had been planning to marry Tim,
But she fell in love with his brother, Jim.
Jim had been thinking of marrying Dee,
But everything changed when he met Marie.

H LISTENING

Listen to each word and then say it.

1. retire
2. memorize
3. practice
4. drug store
5. favorite
6. interrupt
7. around
8. restaurant

9. lively
10. loudly
11. swollen
12. elevator
13. fly
14. believe
15. cold
16. fall asleep

MARYLOU'S BROKEN KEYBOARD

Marylou's keyboard is broken. The r's and the l's don't always work. Fill in the missing r's and l's, and then read Marylou's letters aloud.

1.

Roger,

I'm af_r_aid the__e's something w__ong with the fi__ep__ace in the __iving __oom. A__so, the __ef__ige__ato__ is b__oken. I've been ca__ __ing the __and__o__d fo__ th__ee days on his ce__ __ phone, but he hasn't ca__ __ed back. I hope he ca__ __s me tomo__ __ow.

Ma__y__ou

2.

__ouise,

I'm te__ __ib__y wo__ __ied about my b__othe__ La__ __y's hea__th. He hu__t his __eg whi__e he was p__aying baseba__ __. He had a__ __eady dis__ocated his shou__der whi__e he was su__fing __ast F__iday. Acco__ding to his docto__, he is a__so having p__ob__ems with his b__ood p__essu__e and with his __ight w__ist. He __ea__ __y should t__y to __e__ax and take __ife a __itt__e easie__.

Ma__y__ou

3.

A__no__d,

Can you possib__y __ecommend a good __estau__ant in you__ neighbo__hood? I'm p__anning on taking my re__atives to __unch tomo__ __ow, but I'm not su__e whe__e.

We ate at a ve__y nice G__eek __estau__ant nea__ you__ apa__tment bui__ding __ast month, but I haven't been ab__e to __emembe__ the name. Do you know the p__ace?

You__ f__iend,
Ma__y__ou

4.

__osa,

I have been p__anning a t__ip to F__o__ida. I'__ __ be f__ying to O__ __ando on F__iday, and I'__ __ be __etu__ning th__ee days __ater. Have you eve__ been the__e? I __emembe__ you had fami__y membe__s who __ived in F__o__ida seve__a__ yea__s ago.

P__ease w__ite back.

A__ __ my __ove,
Ma__y__ou

Listen and choose the correct answer.

1. a. He can't find it anywhere.
    b. Where can it be?
    c. Nobody can hear him. *(circled)*

2. a. No, she isn't. She's my wife.
    b. Yes. She's my wife's cousin.
    c. No. She works for a different company.

3. a. Did you take a lot of photographs?
    b. Why did you charge it?
    c. That's too bad. You had been looking forward to it.

4. a. I know. He missed all his tests.
    b. I know. He's been doing very poorly.
    c. I know. He hasn't had a bad grade yet.

5. a. Did she find it?
    b. Whose is it?
    c. I'm sure it hurt a lot.

6. a. We stayed for the lecture.
    b. We talked about classical music.
    c. We read about psychology.

7. a. Did you enjoy yourselves?
    b. How many miles did you travel?
    c. Where did you drive?

8. a. She's having problems with her feet.
    b. She's having problems with her teeth.
    c. That's okay. We all make mistakes.

9. a. Did he make it?
    b. When did you get home?
    c. I know. He likes everything you serve.

10. a. You're right. I bought one.
    b. No, but I heard the noise.
    c. Sorry. We don't sell motorcycles.

11. a. I think so. He's been working hard.
    b. Yes. His plane will leave soon.
    c. I hope so. He never goes to work.

12. a. Poor Amy! She's always sick.
    b. Amy needs a new pair of boots.
    c. She was afraid to ask for it.

13. a. What a shame! Now she can't sing.
    b. What a shame! Now she can't knit.
    c. What a shame! Now she can't walk.

14. a. Would you like to talk about it?
    b. Who are you going to give it to?
    c. What did you decide to do?

15. a. I like you, too.
    b. What are you going to send me?
    c. You don't have anything to be jealous about.

16. a. Was it a very bad accident?
    b. Do you know anybody who can fix it?
    c. How long had they been going out?

17. a. I hope he feels better soon.
    b. What happened? Did you twist it?
    c. How are your cousins?

18. a. Did you call the doctor?
    b. What had you eaten?
    c. Why were you sad?

19. a. I'm glad to hear that.
    b. What was he angry about?
    c. What did he ask them?

20. a. We enjoyed the music.
    b. The lecture was very boring.
    c. The food was excellent.

21. a. They're too small.
    b. You have a job interview today.
    c. You have a baseball game today.

22. a. She enjoys going to the symphony.
    b. She enjoys going window-shopping.
    c. She enjoys doing gymnastics.

23. a. We're going to have a party.
    b. We're going on vacation.
    c. We received a lot of anniversary gifts.

24. a. He's glad he bought it.
    b. He's going to wear it for several years.
    c. He has to return it on Tuesday.

A. Complete the sentences with the appropriate verb form.

(eat)   1. Why do you keep on _____ junk food?

(wrestle) 2. My mother thinks _____ is dangerous.

(stop)   3. I've decided _____ interrupting people all the time.

(box)   4. Bruno practices _____ every day at the gym.

(swim)   5. _____ is a good way to relax.

(skate)   6. Where did your daughter learn _____ so well?

(talk)   7. Please stop _____. I'm trying to sleep!

(do)   8. Rita thinks that _____ exercises is a good way to start the day.

B. Complete the sentences, using the past perfect tense.

Ex. *(wear)*   I wore my favorite striped tie to work yesterday. I ____hadn't worn____ it to work in a long time.

(start)   By the time Andrew got to the play, it ___had___ already ___started___.

(speak)   1. I had dinner with some Japanese friends last night. I enjoyed myself very much

because I _____ Japanese in a long time.

(do)   2. By the time Jennifer's father got home from work, she _____ already

_____ her homework, and she was ready to play baseball in the yard with him.

(leave)   3. Ronald was upset. By the time he got to the train, it _____ already

_____.

(write)   4. I wrote an e-mail to my grandparents last night because I _____ to them for a few weeks.

(have)   5. Patty had pizza for lunch yesterday. She _____ pizza in a long time.

(take)   6. My husband and I took a walk after dinner last night. We _____ a walk after dinner in a long time.

(eat)   7. I ate a big piece of chocolate cake last night and felt terrible about it. I _____

_____ a rich dessert since I started my diet.

(go)   8. My parents went back to their hometown last month. They _____ back there for twenty years.

C.   Complete the sentences, using the past perfect continuous tense.

Ex. *(study)* Jonathan was glad he did well on his astronomy exam. He ___had been studying___ for it for days.

(work) 1. Marvin didn't get his promotion at work. He was heartbroken because he

_____ overtime for several months.

(train) 2. I was disappointed they canceled the marathon last week. I _____

_____ for it since last summer.

(argue) 3. Jane and John broke up last night. They _____ with each other for the past several weeks.

(plan) 4. Nancy caught a cold and couldn't go on her camping trip. It's a shame because she

_____ it since last April.

D.   Listen and choose the correct answer.

Ex. (a.) go fishing.
    b. going canoeing.

1. a. tease her little brother.
    b. interrupting people.

2. a. moving to Miami.
    b. to sell our house.

3. a. to buy a sports car.
    b. buying a sports car.

4. a. waiting in line.
    b. drive downtown.

5. a. going out with Richard.
    b. ask for a raise.

A THE JAMAICAN BOBSLED TEAM

Read the article on student book page 111 and answer the questions.

1. The 1988 Winter Olympic Games were in ____.
   a. Jamaica
   b. Canada
   c. Lake Placid, New York
   d. Norway

2. People were surprised that ____.
   a. Jamaica had a bobsled team
   b. the Jamaican team had poor equipment
   c. the Jamaican team didn't do well
   d. the Jamaican team had trained hard

3. You can infer that most of the Jamaican athletes saw snow for the first time in ____.
   a. Jamaica
   b. Calgary
   c. Lake Placid
   d. Germany

4. In the third paragraph, *give up* means ____.
   a. quit
   b. win
   c. compete
   d. go home

5. To prepare for the 1988 Winter Olympics, the team ____ in Jamaica.
   a. practiced skiing
   b. ran and lifted weights
   c. rode their bobsled
   d. made a movie

6. In 1993 ____.
   a. the Jamaican team did the impossible
   b. the team went back to Calgary
   c. the team arrived in Norway
   d. many people saw a movie about the team

7. In 1994, the Jamaican team came in ____.
   a. tenth in a four-person bobsled
   b. second in a ten-person bobsled
   c. tenth in a two-person bobsled
   d. fourteenth in a two-person bobsled

8. The Jamaican team won the hearts of fans around the world because ____.
   a. they were movie stars
   b. they had done something difficult and unusual
   c. people like Jamaican music
   d. they had won the Olympics

9. The purpose of this article is ____.
   a. to compare Winter and Summer Olympics
   b. to describe Olympic training centers
   c. to explain why Jamaican music is popular
   d. to tell the story of an interesting team of athletes

10. In the bottom left caption under the team's photograph, *part fact and part fiction* means ____.
    a. some parts of the movie are true
    b. some actors in the movie are athletes
    c. they made the movie in Jamaica
    d. they didn't make the movie in Jamaica

B FACT FILE

Look at the Fact File on student book page 113 and answer the questions.

1. ____ countries competed in the Olympics in 1952.
   a. More than one hundred
   b. More than fifty
   c. More than ninety
   d. Between eighty and one hundred

2. About twice as many countries competed in 2000 as in ____.
   a. 1900
   b. 1924
   c. 1952
   d. 1976

C INTERVIEW

Read the interview on student book page 112 and answer the questions.

1. Olga _____ when she was four years old.
   a. moved
   b. had a coach
   c. prepared for a competition
   d. started to skate

2. Olga has been living in the United States _____.
   a. for ten years
   b. since she was seven years old
   c. since she was ten years old
   d. since she met Mr. Abrams

3. Olga won her first medal _____.
   a. seven years ago
   b. before her seventh birthday
   c. after she started to take lessons with Mr. Abrams
   d. after the Regional Competition

4. Olga doesn't take lessons at a skating program in her city because _____.
   a. she doesn't like the teachers
   b. she doesn't like the schedule
   c. she doesn't have time
   d. she has finished all the levels

5. Three months after this interview, Olga is going to compete in the _____.
   a. Regional Figure Skating Competition
   b. National Competition
   c. Summer Olympics
   d. Winter Olympics

6. To prepare for the Regional Figure Skating Competition, Olga trained _____.
   a. seven hours a day
   b. eight hours a day
   c. nine hours a day
   d. ten hours a day

7. When Olga won the Regional Competition, she competed against _____.
   a. women from her part of the country
   b. men and women from her city
   c. women from other countries
   d. women from other parts of the country

8. If Olga does poorly in the National Competition, she _____ in the Olympics next winter.
   a. has to compete
   b. might compete
   c. can't compete
   d. is going to compete

9. When Olga talks about practicing her *routines* over and over again, she is referring to _____.
   a. getting up early
   b. the dances she performs on the ice
   c. her exercises
   d. her medals

10. *Over and over* means _____.
    a. many times
    b. up and down
    c. quickly
    d. slowly

D YOU'RE THE INTERVIEWER!

Imagine you are interviewing a famous athlete! Ask these questions, do some research on the Internet to find the answers, and write the answers below. Then share what you learned with the class.

When did you begin to (play _____, compete in _____)?	
What kind of training do you do?	
What was your best game/competition? Why? How had you prepared for it?	

FUN WITH IDIOMS: What's the Meaning?

Match the expressions and words.

1. Break a ____!   back   Be quiet!

2. Get off my ____!   chin   Don't be sad!

3. Hold your ____!   leg   Don't bother me!

4. Keep your ____ up!   tongue   Pay attention!

5. Put your best ____ forward! eye   Try hard!

6. Keep your ____ on the ball! foot   Good luck!

F **FUN WITH IDIOMS: Finish the Conversations**

Choose the correct expression to complete each conversation.

1. A. I can't believe I made such a stupid mistake!

   B. You weren't paying attention. | Keep your eye on the ball / Keep your chin up |, and it won't happen again.

2. A. I can't stand Mr. Roberts, our math teacher.

   B. | Break a leg! / Hold your tongue! | Here he comes!

3. A. I'm so upset. My husband just lost his job.

   B. Don't worry. | Keep your chin up! / Put your best foot forward! | I'm sure he'll find a new job soon.

4. A. You watch TV all the time, and you never clean your room!

   B. | Keep your eye on the ball / Get off my back |, Charlie! Maybe you should look for a new roommate!

5. A. The play is beginning. I hope I don't forget my lines.

   B. | Hold your tongue! / Break a leg! |

   A. Thanks.

6. A. Tomorrow is the gymnastics competition. I'm a little nervous.

   B. | Get off my back! / Put your best foot forward! | I'm sure you'll be fine.

WE'VE GOT MAIL!

Choose the words that best complete each sentence.

1. Maria ____ to drive.
   a. enjoys
   b. avoids
   c. hates
   d. practices

2. I'm thinking about ____.
   a. get marrying
   b. to get married
   c. getting to marry
   d. getting married

3. I decided ____.
   a. going back to college
   b. to look for a new apartment
   c. time to move to Miami
   d. will start my own business

4. By the time I got to the movie, it ____.
   a. has already started
   b. is already beginning
   c. had already began
   d. had already started

5. I didn't take a vacation in July. I ____ a vacation the month before.
   a. have already been taking
   b. have already taken
   c. had already taken
   d. had already took

6. When my husband got home, I ____ dinner.
   a. had already eaten
   b. already eaten
   c. have already eaten
   d. already eating

Choose the sentence that is correct and complete.

7. a. I'm learning speaking English.
   b. I'm learning to understand English.
   c. I'm learning read English.
   d. I'm learning to writing English.

8. a. He kept on talk all night.
   b. He kept on talking all night.
   c. He kept on to talk all night.
   d. He kept on to talking all night.

9. a. I enjoy to swim at the beach.
   b. I enjoy go swimming at the beach.
   c. I enjoy to go swimming at the beach.
   d. I enjoy swimming at the beach.

10. a. They hadn't went there before.
    b. They didn't went there before.
    c. They hadn't gone there before.
    d. They haven't went there before.

"CAN-DO" REVIEW

Match the "can do" statement and the correct sentence.

____ 1. I can introduce myself.

____ 2. I can agree with someone.

____ 3. I can describe my feelings and emotions.

____ 4. I can express appreciation.

____ 5. I can offer advice.

____ 6. I can describe an accomplishment.

____ 7. I can describe forgetting to do something.

____ 8. I can react to bad news.

____ 9. I can ask if someone agrees.

____ 10. I can report household repair problems.

a. That's very nice of you.

b. Our water heater hasn't been working.

c. I passed my driver's test yesterday.

d. You're right.

e. Don't you think so?

f. That's terrible!

g. Hi. My name is Daniel.

h. I think you should start your own business.

i. I'm nervous.

j. I had forgotten to turn off my computer.

1. A. Did you pick up Rover at the vet?

   B. No. I didn't _____pick him up_____.
   I thought YOU did.

2. A. Did you turn on the heat?

   B. Yes. I _____ a few
   hours ago, but it's still cold in here.

3. A. You should take back these library
   books.

   B. I know. I'll _____
   tomorrow morning.

4. A. Has Diane filled out her income tax
   forms?

   B. No. She's going to _____
   this weekend.

5. A. Where should we hang up this
   portrait?

   B. Let's _____
   over the fireplace.

6. A. I'm having trouble hooking up my
   computer.

   B. No problem. I'll _____.

7. A. Are you ever going to throw out these
   old souvenirs?

   B. I'll _____
   some day.

8. A. Did Sally take back her cell phone to
   the store?

   B. Yes. She _____
   this afternoon.

9. A. Did your daughter take down the
   photographs of her old boyfriend?

   B. Yes. She _____
   as soon as they stopped going out.

10. A. Did you remember to call up Aunt
    Clara to wish her "Happy Birthday"?

    B. Sorry. I didn't _____.
    I forgot it was her birthday.

| bring back | hand in | put away | put on | take off | turn off | turn on | wake up |

1. I think we should __turn on__ the air conditioner. It's getting very hot in here.

   Good idea. I'll _____ right away.

2. When are you going to __hand__ your biology report __in__?

   I'm going to _____ tomorrow morning. I have to write it tonight.

3. Let's _____ Mom and Dad! It's 8:00, and they're still sleeping!

   Don't _____. It's Saturday. They don't go to work today.

4. Don't forget to _____ the printer _____ before you leave the office tonight.

   You don't have to worry. I always _____ before I leave.

5. Why don't you _____ your hat and coat? It's warm in here.

   I'll _____ in a few minutes. I'm still a little cold.

6. Susie, when are you going to _____ your toys _____?

   I'm still playing with them. I'll _____ later.

7. Teddy, it's time for bed. _____ your pajamas _____!

   Okay, Dad. I'll _____ in a few minutes.

8. Do you think Richard will _____ his girlfriend _____ to the house after the dance?

   I don't know. Maybe he'll _____. I hope he does. I really want to meet her.

C GRAMMARRAP: *I Don't Know How!*

Listen. Then clap and practice.

A.　Take off your　　skis.

　　Take them off　now!

B.　I can't take them　off.

　　I don't know　how!

A.　Turn off the　　engine!

　　Turn it off　now!

B.　I can't turn it　off.

　　I don't know　how!

A.　Turn on the　　oven!

　　Turn it on　now!

B.　I can't turn it　on.

　　I don't know　how!

A.　Hook up the　　printer!

　　Hook it up　now!

B.　I can't hook it　up.

　　I don't know　how!

A.　Pick up the　　suitcase.

　　Give it to　　Jack.

B.　I can't pick it　up.

　　I have　　a bad back!

A.　Take back　　the videos!

　　Take them back today.

B.　I can't take them　back.

　　It's a holiday!

WHAT ARE THEY SAYING?

cross out	give back	look up	throw away	turn off
do over	hook up	think over	turn down	write down

1. Did your teacher like the composition you wrote about Australian birds?

   No, she didn't. I have to ___*do it over*___.

2. A. Do we still have the hammer we borrowed from our next-door neighbors?

   B. No, we don't. We _____ a long time ago.

3. A. What's the matter with the answering machine? Is it broken?

   B. No, it isn't. I forgot to _____.

4. A. Are you going to accept the invitation to Roger's wedding?

   B. I don't know. I have to _____ carefully. His wedding is in Alaska.

5. A. What's the weather forecast for tomorrow?

   B. I'm not sure. You should _____ on the Internet.

6. A. Is Kimberly going to the prom with Frank?

   B. No, she isn't. She had to _____ because she already had a date with somebody else.

7. A. What should I do with all these letters from my ex-boyfriend?

   B. I think you should _____.

8. A. What's Walter's new address?

   B. I can't remember. But I know I've _____ somewhere.

9. A. Should I erase all these mistakes in my math homework?

   B. No, I think you should just _____.

10. Why aren't you watching the president's speech on TV?

    I watched it for a while, but it was boring. So I

    _____.

E WHAT'S THE WORD?

James just moved into a new apartment. What does he have to do?

1. He has to ~~put away~~ / throw away his books and his clothes.

2. He has to fill out / hook up his printer and his computer.

3. He has to take out / take back the moving truck he rented.

Jennifer is very happy and excited. She just got engaged. What's she going to do?

4. She's going to wake up / drop off her parents and tell them the news.

5. She's going to call off / call up all her friends.

6. She's going to look up / write down all the things her boyfriend said.

Mr. and Mrs. Baker's aunt and uncle are going to visit them next week. What do the Bakers have to do before then?

7. They have to clean up / take out their apartment.

8. They have to pick out / put away their children's toys.

9. They have to throw out / hook up all their old newspapers.

10. They have to call up / hang up their aunt and uncle's portrait.

F WHAT SHOULD THEY DO?

figure out	look up	throw out	use up
give back	think over	turn off	wake up

1.
Abigail, will you marry me?

That's a big decision, Howard.
I have to _____think it over_____.

2. A. I've been using my neighbor's screwdriver all summer.

   B. Don't you think it's time to _____?

3. A. Is there any more sugar?

   B. No. We _____. We have to buy some tomorrow.

4. A. I don't know the definition of this word.

   B. You really should _____ in the dictionary.

5. A. This math problem is very difficult.

   B. Maybe your mother can help you _____.

6. A. It's 7:30, and the children are still sleeping.

   B. They're going to be late for school. I'll _____.

7. A. It's really cold in here! Is the air conditioner on?

   B. Yes, it is. I'll _____ right away.

8. A. I'm very embarrassed. These are the worst photographs anyone has ever taken of me.

   B. Well, if they bother you that much, why don't you _____?

G LISTENING

Listen and choose the correct answer.

1. a. picked it up.
   b. used it up.

2. a. turn it down.
   b. turn it on.

3. a. take them down.
   b. turn them down.

4. a. think them over.
   b. drop them off.

5. a. hook it up.
   b. look it up.

6. a. give it back?
   b. hand it in?

7. a. throw it out.
   b. figure it out.

8. a. write it down.
   b. use it up.

9. a. pick it up.
   b. clean it up.

H COME UP WITH THE RIGHT ANSWER

call on	get over	look through	pick on	take after
get along with	hear from	look up to	run into	

1. I _____take after_____ my father. We're both athletic, we're both interested in engineering, and we both like to paint. I'm really

glad I _____take after him_____ .

2. I haven't _____ my son in three weeks. He's

at college, and I usually _____ every week!

3. I'm so embarrassed. My teacher _____ me twice in class today, but I didn't know ANY of the answers. I have to study

tonight. She might _____ again tomorrow.

4. My husband and I enjoyed _____ our wedding

pictures. We hadn't _____ in years.

5. Jack _____ his cold very quickly. I think he

_____ fast because he stayed home and took care of himself.

6. I really _____ my grandmother. She's honest, she's intelligent, and she's very generous. I hope someday when I'm a

grandmother, my grandchildren will _____, too.

7. I was very surprised. I _____ my old girlfriend at the

bank yesterday morning. And then I _____ again at a movie last night.

8. I don't _____ my mother-in-law. We often

disagree. All the people in our family _____. Why can't I?

9. Bobby is mean. He _____ his cats all the time.

The cats don't like it when Bobby _____.

Listen. Then clap and practice.

I don't   get along with   Kate and   Clem.

I almost   never   hear from   them.

But I get along   well   with Bob   and Fay.

I call them   up   three times   a day.

Jack   takes after   his Uncle   Jim.

Bob   looks up to   his father,   Tim.

Kate never   picks on   her sister,   Sue.

But she always   picks on   her brother,   Lou.

J CHOOSE

1. A. Do we have any more pens?
    B. No, we don't. We _____.
       a. ran into them
       b. ran out of them *(circled)*

2. A. Does Carol still have the flu?
    B. No. She _____ a few days ago.
       a. got over it
       b. got it over

3. A. Does Jill get along with her brother?
    B. No. He _____ all the time.
       a. picks her on
       b. picks on her

4. A. I can't remember Tom's phone number.
    B. You should _____.
       a. look up to him
       b. look it up

5. A. Amy knows all the answers in class.
    B. Does the teacher always _____?
       a. call on her
       b. call her on

6. A. This is a very difficult problem.
    B. I know. I can't _____.
       a. figure out it
       b. figure it out

7. A. Have you heard from Pam recently?
    B. Yes. I _____ the other day.
       a. heard her from
       b. heard from her

8. A. What should I do with these old letters?
    B. Why don't you _____?
       a. throw them out
       b. throw out them

9. A. These photographs are wonderful!
    B. I know. Let's _____ again.
       a. look through them
       b. look them through

10. A. Do you like William?
    B. Oh, yes. I _____ very well.
       a. get him along
       b. get along with him

11. A. Should I turn off the computer?
    B. No. You can _____.
       a. leave it on
       b. leave on it

12. A. Did you hang up your uncle's portrait?
    B. No, I didn't. I _____.
       a. took it down
       b. took down it

13. A. You look like your father.
    B. I know. Everybody says I _____.
       a. take him after
       b. take after him

14. A. They have a very unusual last name.
    B. You'll remember it if you _____.
       a. write down it
       b. write it down

WHAT DOES IT MEAN?

Choose the correct answer.

1. Richard takes after his mother.
   a. He's always with her.
   b. They're both shy. *(circled)*
   c. His mother always arrives first.

2. Please turn off the air conditioner.
   a. It's too hot in this room.
   b. The room is too small.
   c. It's too cold in this room.

3. Tom left his briefcase on the plane.
   a. Maybe his mind slipped.
   b. He forgot it.
   c. He was very careful.

4. I'm going to take these pants back.
   a. They're new.
   b. They're medium.
   c. They're too baggy.

5. Fran can't find her notebook.
   a. I hope she didn't throw it out.
   b. I hope she didn't fill it out.
   c. I hope she didn't take it off.

6. Bob doesn't get along with his neighbors.
   a. He can't stand to talk to them.
   b. He likes them very much.
   c. He looks up to them.

7. I hope I don't run into my old boyfriend.
   a. Why? Will he get hurt?
   b. Why don't you want to see him?
   c. Why? Does he like to jog?

8. Paul had to do his homework over.
   a. It was excellent.
   b. He didn't think it over.
   c. He had made a lot of mistakes.

 LISTENING

Listen and choose the correct answer.

1. a. He's very tall.
   b. I can never find him.
   c. I want to be like him. *(circled)*

2. a. You're lucky he has a car.
   b. I'm sure that bothers you.
   c. Do you also pick him up?

3. a. Yes. I put it in the closet.
   b. Yes. I gave it to our neighbor.
   c. Yes. We had used it all up.

4. a. I'm sorry you're still sick.
   b. I'm glad you're feeling better.
   c. It's too bad you have to do it over.

5. a. No. He speaks very softly.
   b. Yes. He sent me an e-mail yesterday.
   c. No. I haven't heard him recently.

6. a. The music was very loud.
   b. Somebody had picked it up.
   c. I already had another date.

7. a. Yes, several times.
   b. Yes, but I wasn't home.
   c. Yes, but I had already left the house.

8. a. He didn't need it anymore.
   b. It was already at the cleaner's.
   c. I know. He found one he really liked.

9. a. Did she hurt herself?
   b. How did you hurt yourself?
   c. When does her plane leave?

10. a. The store isn't having a sale.
    b. Everything in the store is cheaper.
    c. Everything is 20 cents less this week.

11. a. Good. I'll buy it.
    b. Don't worry. We have larger ones.
    c. I know. It's too tight.

12. a. Yes. I used up four pair.
    b. Yes. I put on four pair.
    c. Yes. I looked up four pair.

1. I ate too much.   So ___did I___.

2. I hate to go to the mall.   _____, too.

3. I can play the trombone.   So _____.

4. I'm allergic to milk.   _____, too.

5. I'll be starting college this fall.   _____, too.

6. I was late for work.   So _____.

7. I'm going to retire soon.   So _____.

8. I've been doing poorly in school recently.   _____, too.

9. I just got a promotion.   _____, too.

10. I'll be on vacation next week.   So _____.

11. I have to lose a little weight.   So _____.

Activity Workbook **109**

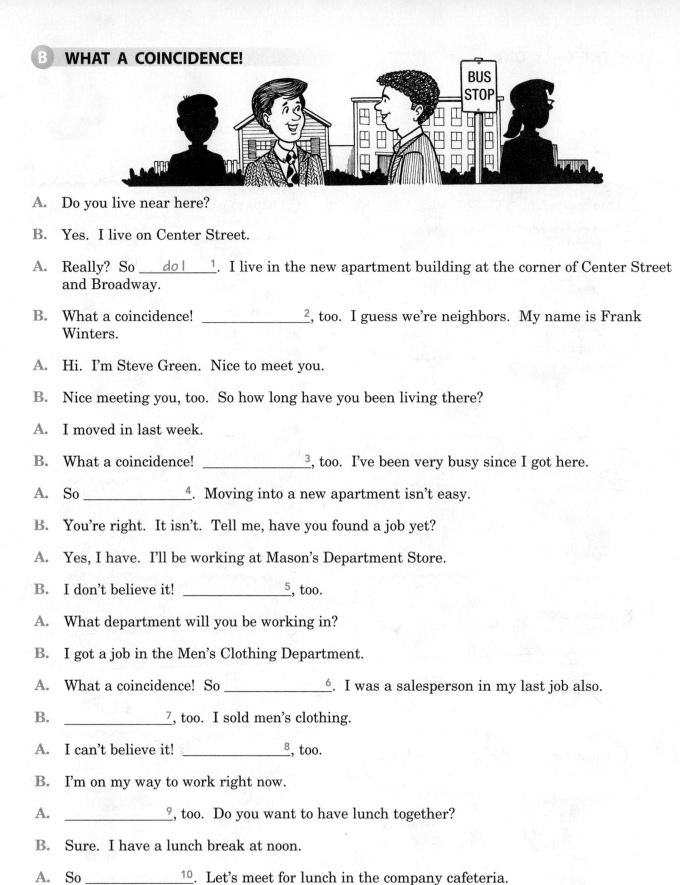

A. Do you live near here?

B. Yes. I live on Center Street.

A. Really? So ___do I___[1]. I live in the new apartment building at the corner of Center Street and Broadway.

B. What a coincidence! _____[2], too. I guess we're neighbors. My name is Frank Winters.

A. Hi. I'm Steve Green. Nice to meet you.

B. Nice meeting you, too. So how long have you been living there?

A. I moved in last week.

B. What a coincidence! _____[3], too. I've been very busy since I got here.

A. So _____[4]. Moving into a new apartment isn't easy.

B. You're right. It isn't. Tell me, have you found a job yet?

A. Yes, I have. I'll be working at Mason's Department Store.

B. I don't believe it! _____[5], too.

A. What department will you be working in?

B. I got a job in the Men's Clothing Department.

A. What a coincidence! So _____[6]. I was a salesperson in my last job also.

B. _____[7], too. I sold men's clothing.

A. I can't believe it! _____[8], too.

B. I'm on my way to work right now.

A. _____[9], too. Do you want to have lunch together?

B. Sure. I have a lunch break at noon.

A. So _____[10]. Let's meet for lunch in the company cafeteria.

B. Okay. That'll be nice. I'm looking forward to it.

A. So _____[11].

1. I didn't like the movie.
   Neither _____did I_____.

2. I'm not feeling very well.
   _____ either.

3. I wasn't in school yesterday.
   Neither _____.

4. I can't play tennis very well.
   _____ either.

5. I won't be home tonight.
   _____ either.

6. I've never been in the hospital before.
   Neither _____.

7. I can't stand driving in traffic.
   _____ either.

8. I'm not going to order dessert.
   Neither _____.

9. I didn't enjoy the lecture.
   _____ either.

10. I don't like to practice the piano.
    Neither _____.

11. I'll never go sailing again.
    Neither _____.

Listen and complete the sentences.

1. So _____did I_____ .

2. _____ , too.

3. So _____ .

4. _____ either.

5. _____ , too.

6. _____ , too.

7. Neither _____ .

8. _____ , too.

9. Neither _____ .

10. So _____ .

11. _____ either.

12. _____ , too.

13. Neither _____ .

14. So _____ .

15. _____ either.

E GRAMMARRAP: *So Do I*

Listen. Then clap and practice.

A.   I like to   fly.

B.   So do   I.

A.   They like to   ski.

B.   So do   we.

A.   She likes the   zoo.

B.   He does,   too.

A.   You're a good   friend.

B.   So are   you.

F GRAMMARRAP: *They Didn't Either*

Listen. Then clap and practice.

We didn't   eat it.

They didn't   either.

He didn't   finish it.

Neither did   she.

She wasn't   hungry.

He wasn't   either.

They weren't   hungry.

Neither were   we.

G   WHAT ARE THEY SAYING?

1. Why were you and your brother late for school today?

   I had to go to the dentist, and so ____did he____.

2. Will you and your wife be home this evening?

   I don't think so. I'll be working late, and so _____.

3. How did you and Tom feel after you ran in the marathon?

   I was exhausted, and _____, too.

4. Would you and your sister like to learn how to ski?

   Actually, I've already tried it, and so _____.

5. Can Ricky and I go to the movies tonight?

   He should study for his English exam, and _____, too.

6. Have you seen Mr. and Mrs. Martinez recently?

   I saw them today. I was in the park, and _____, too.

7. Should I go into the water with Timmy and Susie?

   No. That's okay. Timmy can swim, and _____ Susie.

8. Why weren't you and your brother at baseball practice today?

   I had to help my mother, and so _____.

9. Why are you and your wife leaving the party?

   She has to get up early tomorrow, and _____, too.

10. Why are your parents so worried?

    I've decided to ....
    ....,
    and .... my brother.

1. Are you and your brother going to be in the school play?

   Unfortunately, he can't act, and neither _____can I_____.

2. Why do you and your friends look so upset?

   I didn't do very well on the math test, and _____ either.

3. Did you and your son see the baseball game on TV today?

   No, we didn't. I'm not interested in sports, and neither _____.

4. Are you and your sister going to go to the concert tonight?

   No, we aren't. I don't like folk music, and _____ either.

5. Why did you and your friends leave the dance so early last night?

   I wasn't having a very good time, and neither _____.

6. Have you and your wife made plans for your vacation yet?

   I haven't had very much time, and _____ either.

7. Are you and your roommates going to Sally's wedding?

   No, we aren't. I won't be here this weekend, and neither _____.

8. It's getting late. Should I make dinner now?

   The truth is, I'm not very hungry, and the children _____.

9. Is the DVD player still broken?

   Yes, it is. I haven't been able to fix it, and _____ your father.

10. How was your date with Samantha last night?

    We were both a little nervous. I had never gone out on a date before, and _____ either.

so	too	either	neither

1. A. Why didn't Ronald and his wife go to work yesterday?

   B. He had a terrible cold,

   and {
   _____ so did she _____.
   _____ she did, too _____.
   }

3. A. Do Jack and his girlfriend enjoy going sailing?

   B. No, they don't. She gets seasick,

   and {
   _____.
   _____.
   }

5. A. Why did Beverly and Brian have trouble doing their chemistry experiments?

   B. He hadn't followed the instructions,

   and {
   _____.
   _____.
   }

2. A. Did Betty and Bob enjoy the concert last night?

   B. Not really. She couldn't hear the music,

   and {
   _____.
   _____.
   }

4. A. Why didn't Mr. and Mrs. Miller order the cheesecake for dessert?

   B. He doesn't eat rich foods,

   and {
   _____.
   _____.
   }

6. A. Why aren't you and Peter good friends any more?

   B. I'm in love with Amanda Richardson,

   and {
   _____.
   _____.
   }

1. I'm tall, but my sister and brother _____aren't_____. I've always _____ the tallest person in our family.

2. My brother isn't very athletic, but my sister _____. She enjoys _____ squash and _____ gymnastics.

3. I can't draw pictures, but my brother _____. He's been _____ pictures since he _____ four years old.

4. My brother and I have different interests. I enjoy seeing movies, but my brother _____. He enjoys _____ to lectures and concerts.

5. My mother is interested in photography, but my father _____. My mother _____ photographs since she was a teenager.

6. My father has lived here all his life, but his parents _____. They've _____ in this country _____ fifty years. Before that, they _____ in Italy.

7. My grandparents sometimes speak to us in Italian, but my father _____. He _____ Italian to anyone in a long time.

8. I'll be going to college next year, but my brother _____. He _____ finished high school yet.

9. I don't have a very good voice, but my sister _____. She sings in the school choir. She has _____ in the choir _____ she started high school.

10. I'm usually very neat, but my sister and brother _____. They never hang _____ their clothes or put _____ their books.

11. I know how to ski, but my brother _____. I've been skiing _____ the past nine years.

12. My sister is a very good skater, but my brother and I _____. We just started _____ a month ago. Before that, we _____ never _____ at all.

K LISTENING

Listen and complete the sentences.

1. but my husband _____ *didn't* _____ .
2. but my daughter _____ .
3. but you _____ .
4. but I _____ .
5. but my friends _____ .
6. but my wife _____ .
7. but you _____ .
8. but my brother _____ .
9. but everybody else _____ .
10. but our teacher _____ .
11. but my son _____ .
12. but the other man _____ .
13. but my sister _____ .
14. but I _____ .
15. but my friends _____ .
16. but my brother _____ .
17. but my children _____ .
18. but I _____ .

L GRAMMARRAP: *I've Been Working Hard, and You Have, Too*

Listen. Then clap and practice.

I've been working hard, and   you have,   too.
I'm   exhausted,   and so   are you.
He's been   out of town,   and so   has she.
They've been very   busy,   and so   have we.

I   didn't go,   and neither   did he.
They   weren't there,   and neither   were we.
We   stayed home,   and so   did they.
Nobody   went   to the meeting   that day.

I don't speak   Greek,   but my brother   does.
I wasn't born in   Greece,   but my mother   was.
I didn't study   Greek,   but my brother   did.
He's spoken   Greek   since he was   a kid.

Activity Workbook   117

SOUND IT OUT! 🔊

Listen to each word and then say it.

f<u>u</u>ll		f<u>oo</u>l

	f<u>u</u>ll				f<u>oo</u>l	
1.	l<u>oo</u>k	3.	p<u>u</u>t	1.	n<u>oo</u>n	3.	J<u>u</u>dy
2.	c<u>ou</u>ld	4.	f<u>oo</u>t	2.	dr<u>ew</u>	4.	f<u>oo</u>d

Listen and put a circle around the word that has the same sound.

1. f<u>u</u>ll: p<u>oo</u>l   (c<u>oo</u>ks)   sh<u>oe</u>

2. fl<u>u</u>:   t<u>oo</u>   w<u>ou</u>ld   bl<u>oo</u>d

3. g<u>oo</u>d: s<u>ou</u>p   sh<u>ou</u>ldn't   J<u>u</u>ne

4. w<u>oo</u>d: fl<u>u</u>   t<u>oo</u>th   p<u>u</u>t

5. c<u>ou</u>ld: c<u>u</u>p   c<u>oo</u>kies   <u>u</u>pstairs

6. h<u>oo</u>k: f<u>oo</u>d   m<u>o</u>vie   g<u>oo</u>d

7. w<u>o</u>man: s<u>u</u>gar   tr<u>u</u>e   n<u>ew</u>

Now make a sentence using all the words you circled, and read the sentence aloud.

8. .... much ....

   in their ....

9. s<u>ui</u>t: tw<u>o</u>   p<u>u</u>t   b<u>u</u>s

10. c<u>oo</u>k: f<u>oo</u>d   b<u>oo</u>ks   s<u>u</u>nny

11. f<u>oo</u>t: b<u>oo</u>kcase   p<u>oo</u>l   m<u>u</u>st

12. bl<u>u</u>e: j<u>u</u>st   wh<u>o</u>   l<u>oo</u>ked

13. w<u>ou</u>ld: s<u>ui</u>t   t<u>oo</u>l   t<u>oo</u>k

14. c<u>oo</u>l: st<u>oo</u>d   aftern<u>oo</u>n   p<u>u</u>lse

15. sch<u>oo</u>l: S<u>u</u>san's   th<u>u</u>nder   fl<u>oo</u>r

Now make a sentence using all the words you circled, and read the sentence aloud.

16. .... from ....

   .... this .... ?

WHAT DOES IT MEAN?

_j_	1.	afford	a.	afraid
	2.	argue	b.	do poorly
	3.	bachelor	c.	fight
	4.	begin	d.	finish
	5.	bump into	e.	friendly and talkative
	6.	can't stand	f.	give back
	7.	compatible	g.	give lessons
	8.	consider	h.	hate
	9.	continue	i.	have a lot in common
	10.	discuss	j.	have enough money
	11.	exam	k.	how much it costs
	12.	exhausted	l.	hurt
	13.	fail	m.	keep on
	14.	frightened	n.	meet
	15.	hike	o.	ready
	16.	injure	p.	recently
	17.	lately	q.	single man
	18.	outgoing	r.	someone who doesn't eat meat
	19.	prepared	s.	start
	20.	price	t.	study again
	21.	return	u.	take a long walk
	22.	review	v.	talk about
	23.	stand in line	w.	test
	24.	teach	x.	think about
	25.	use up	y.	tired
	26.	vegetarian	z.	wait

A. Complete the sentences.

Ex. My son is waiting for me at the bus stop. I have to pick ___him___ ___up___ right away.

My mother and I are both tall with curly hair. Everybody says I take ___after___ ___her___.

1. I'll finish my homework in a little while, and then I'll hand _____ _____.

2. My father is a very smart man. I really look _____ _____ _____.

3. I haven't talked to Aunt Shirley lately. I hope I hear _____ _____ soon.

4. My English teacher didn't like my composition. I have to do _____ _____.

5. I don't know the definition of this word. I need to look _____ _____.

6. I can't find any flour. I think we ran _____ _____ _____.

7. I can't find my wallet. Could you help me look _____ _____?

8. Don't leave your clothes on the bed. You really should hang _____ _____.

9. Don't worry about your mistakes. You can always cross _____ _____.

10. I can never remember Alan's address. I should write _____ _____.

11. I've had the flu for the past several days. My doctor says I'll get _____ _____ soon.

B. Complete the sentences.

so	too	neither	either

Ex. Maria did well on her science test, and ___so did___ her sister.

1. I'm wearing new shoes today, and _____ my brother.

2. I won't be able to come to the meeting tomorrow, and _____ Barbara.

3. I was bored during Professor Gray's lecture, and my friends _____.

4. Janet can't skate, and her brother _____.

5. I've been taking guitar lessons for years, and _____ my sisters.

6. David worked overtime yesterday, and his wife _____.

7. Louise has never been to Europe, and _____ her husband.

8. I want to complain to the landlord, and _____ my neighbors.

9. I'm not very athletic, and _____ my wife.

C. Listen and complete the sentences.

Ex. but her husband _____*doesn't*_____.

1. but my sister _____.

2. but my parents _____.

3. but my brother _____.

4. but my wife _____.

5. but I _____.

Read the article on student book page 145 and answer the questions.

1. In a traditional Indian family, _____.
    a. the mother finds a husband for her daughter
    b. the father finds a husband for his daughter
    c. the daughter finds her own husband
    d. a matchmaker finds a husband for the daughter

2. A traditional Indian family wants their daughter to marry a man who _____.
    a. has a good job
    b. is an astrologer
    c. met their daughter at school
    d. reads horoscopes

3. Families hire astrologers to _____.
    a. find out when their child was born
    b. introduce young people to each other
    c. predict if a young man and woman are good for each other
    d. arrange a marriage

4. An astrologer approves a match if the man and woman _____.
    a. fall in love
    b. have the same interests
    c. have good occupations
    d. have birth dates and times that are a good match

5. People who use dating services probably don't _____.
    a. answer questions about their interests
    b. submit a photograph
    c. submit a horoscope
    d. answer questions about their education

6. In the fourth paragraph, *submit* means to _____.
    a. buy   c. take
    b. copy   d. send in

7. Many young people put personal ads in newspapers because _____.
    a. it's a family tradition
    b. they want to meet someone
    c. they want to hire a matchmaker
    d. they want to save money

8. You can infer that marriages that parents arrange _____.
    a. are becoming less common
    b. are happier than other marriages
    c. don't last as long as other marriages
    d. are more common in cities than in rural areas

9. The purpose of this article is _____.
    a. to recommend ways to meet people
    b. to give advice to young people
    c. to describe traditions and customs in different parts of the world
    d. to warn about matchmakers and astrologers

10. A key detail that supports the main idea of the article is _____.
    a. astrologers in India read a young man's horoscope to decide if there is a good match
    b. dating services are more popular than before
    c. matchmakers are common in rural areas
    d. some parents arrange marriages before children are born

B **FACT FILE**

Look at the Fact File on student book page 145 and answer the questions.

1. Women in Japan usually get married _____ than women in Mexico.
    a. four years later   c. six years later
    b. five years later   d. seven years later

2. Women in Swaziland usually get married 12 years earlier than women in _____.
    a. Saudi Arabia   c. Japan
    b. Australia   d. Sweden

AROUND THE WORLD

Read the article on student book page 146 and answer the questions.

1. Brides often wear _____ on their heads.
   a. a bouquet
   b. confetti
   c. a veil
   d. a helmet

2. A _____ is NOT a place of worship.
   a. mosque
   b. reception hall
   c. temple
   d. church

3. A public wedding _____.
   a. is always outdoors
   b. is very short
   c. doesn't have many guests
   d. is for everybody in the neighborhood

4. The groom in the Hindu ceremony is wearing _____.
   a. a veil
   b. a crown
   c. a bowtie
   d. a tuxedo

5. People do NOT shower the bride and groom with _____ for good luck.
   a. confetti
   b. flower petals
   c. water
   d. rice

6. A wedding procession is _____.
   a. a parade
   b. wedding music
   c. a traditional dance
   d. a special food

7. In Cyprus, _____.
   a. the guests throw money at the bride and groom
   b. the bride and groom give the guests money
   c. the bride gives money to the groom
   d. the guests attach money to the bride and groom's clothes

8. The bride and groom in Colombia _____.
   a. are putting candles in a cake
   b. are lighting candles
   c. are making a wish
   d. are singing a song

9. In the United States, the bride throws _____.
   a. rice
   b. confetti
   c. a bouquet
   d. flower petals

10. According to tradition, the person who catches the bouquet will _____.
    a. have good luck
    b. light a candle
    c. cut the cake
    d. get married next

INTERVIEW

Read the Interviews on student book page 147 and answer the questions.

1. The couple who paid to meet each other met _____.
   a. at a bookstore
   b. at work
   c. through a dating service
   d. in college

2. *High school sweethearts* are _____.
   a. high school friends
   b. high school classmates
   c. high school teammates
   d. a boyfriend and girlfriend in high school

3. The youngest couple to start going out together was probably the couple who _____.
   a. met through a dating service
   b. were high school sweethearts
   c. met at work
   d. met in college

4. On a *blind date,* _____.
   a. you wear a mask
   b. you close your eyes
   c. you go out with someone you have never met before
   d. you talk on the telephone

E FUN WITH IDIOMS

Choose the best response.

1. George gave me the cold shoulder.
   a. Did you see a doctor?
   b. I'm surprised. I thought he liked you.
   c. What are you going to give him?
   d. That's nice.

2. I'm nuts about Sally.
   a. I don't like her either.
   b. You shouldn't be angry at her.
   c. What's wrong with her?
   d. You should tell her. I think she likes you, too.

3. Rosa stood me up.
   a. There weren't any seats left.
   b. She's very helpful.
   c. Maybe she had to work late.
   d. Did you enjoy your date?

4. I fell for Harry the moment I met him.
   a. Really? So quickly?
   b. What a terrible way to meet someone!
   c. When did you start to like him?
   d. He's very clumsy.

F WE'VE GOT MAIL!

Choose the words that best complete each sentence.

1. Wake _____ at 8:00.
   a. up me
   b. up him
   c. up them
   d. up your sister

2. When are you going to _____?
   a. put away them
   b. hang up them
   c. hear from them
   d. drop off them

3. Think _____.
   a. it over
   b. it around
   c. it about
   d. over it

4. Don't _____.
   a. pick your brother on
   b. pick him on
   c. pick on him
   d. pick up him

5. Did you _____?
   a. hand in it
   b. look for it
   c. do over it
   d. figure out it

6. Rita takes _____.
   a. out it
   b. off it
   c. me after
   d. after her father

G "CAN-DO" REVIEW

Match the "can do" statement and the correct sentence.

_____ 1. I can give information about myself.

_____ 2. I can give advice.

_____ 3. I can express inability.

_____ 4. I can express obligation.

_____ 5. I can tell about future plans.

_____ 6. I can describe things that haven't occurred yet.

_____ 7. I can compare myself with another person.

_____ 8. I can describe a person's background.

_____ 9. I can describe a person's personality.

_____ 10. I can invite someone to do something.

a. I'd like to, but I can't.

b. I've never done that.

c. He's a very quiet person.

d. I'm going to wash my car tomorrow.

e. Would you like to see a movie with me today?

f. I'm a vegetarian.

g. My mother was born in a small town in Portugal.

h. I think you should do it over.

i. My brother and I are very different.

j. I have to clean up my apartment.

Listening Scripts

Page 7 Exercise H
Listen to each question and then complete the answer.

1. Does Jim like to play soccer?
2. Is Alice working today?
3. Are those students staying after school today?
4. Do Mr. and Mrs. Jackson work hard?
5. Does your wife still write poetry?
6. Is it raining?
7. Is he busy?
8. Do you have to leave?
9. Does your sister play the violin?
10. Is your brother studying in the library?
11. Are you wearing a necklace today?
12. Do you and your husband go camping very often?
13. Is your niece doing her homework?
14. Are they still chatting online?
15. Do you and your friends play Scrabble very often?

Page 13 Exercise B
Listen and circle the correct answer.

1. They work.
2. They worked.
3. We study English.
4. I waited for the bus.
5. We visit our friends.
6. She met important people.
7. He taught Chinese.
8. She delivers the mail.
9. I wrote letters to my friends.
10. I ride my bicycle to work.
11. He sleeps very well.
12. I had a terrible headache.

Page 26 Exercise C
Listen and choose the time of the action.

1. My daughter is going to sing Broadway show tunes in her high school show.
2. Janet bought a new dress for her friend's party.
3. Are you going to go out with George?
4. I went shopping at the new mall.
5. How did you poke yourself in the eye?
6. Who's going to prepare dinner?
7. Did the baby sleep well?
8. I'm really looking forward to Saturday night.
9. Is your son going to play games on his computer?
10. We're going to complain to the landlord about the heat in our apartment.
11. We bought a dozen donuts.
12. I'm going to take astronomy.

Page 33 Exercise L
Listen to each story. Then answer the questions.
What Are Mr. and Mrs. Miller Looking Forward to?

Mr. and Mrs. Miller moved into their new house in Los Angeles last week. They're happy because the house has a large, bright living room and a big, beautiful yard. They're looking forward to life in their new home. Every weekend they'll be able to relax in their living room and enjoy the beautiful California weather in their big, beautiful yard. But this weekend Mr. and Mrs. Miller won't be relaxing. They're going to be very busy. First, they're going to repaint the living room. Then, they're going to assemble their new

computer and VCR. And finally, they're going to plant some flowers in their yard. They'll finally be able to relax NEXT weekend.

What's Jonathan Looking Forward to?

I'm so excited! I'm sitting at my computer in my office, but I'm not thinking about my work today. I'm thinking about next weekend because next Saturday is the day I'll be getting married. After the wedding, my wife and I will be going to Hawaii for a week. I can't wait! For one week, we won't be working, we won't be cooking, we won't be cleaning, and we won't be paying bills. We'll be swimming in the ocean, relaxing on the beach, and eating in fantastic restaurants.

What's Mrs. Grant Looking Forward to?

Mrs. Grant is going to retire this year, and she's really looking forward to her new life. She won't be getting up early every morning and taking the bus to work. She'll be able to sleep late every day of the week. She'll read books, she'll work in her garden, and she'll go to museums with her friends. And she's very happy that she'll be able to spend more time with her grandchildren. She'll take them to the park to feed the birds, she'll take them to the zoo to see the animals, and she'll baby-sit when her son and daughter-in-law go out on Saturday nights.

Page 35 Exercise E
Listen to each question and then complete the answer.

Ex. Does your brother like to swim?
1. Are you going to buy donuts tomorrow?
2. Will Jennifer and John see each other again soon?
3. Doctor, did I sprain my ankle?
4. Does Tommy have a black eye?
5. Is your daughter practicing the violin?
6. Do you and your husband go to the movies very often?
7. Does Diane go out with her boyfriend every Saturday evening?
8. Will you and your wife be visiting us tonight?

Page 36 Exercise B
Listen and choose the word you hear.

1. I've ridden them for many years.
2. Yes. I've taken French.
3. I'm giving injections.
4. I've driven one for many years.
5. Yes. I've written it.
6. I'm drawing it right now.
7. I've spoken it for many years.
8. Yes. I've drawn that.

Page 37 Exercise D
Is Speaker B answering Yes or No? Listen to each conversation and circle the correct answer.

1. A. Do you know how to drive a bus?
   B. I've driven a bus for many years.
2. A. I usually take the train to work. Do you also take the train?
   B. Actually, I've never taken the train to work.
3. A. Are you a good swimmer?
   B. To tell the truth, I've never swum very well.
4. A. Did you get up early this morning?
   B. I've gotten up early every morning this week.

(continued)

5. A. I'm going to give my dog a bath today. Do you have any advice?
   B. Sorry. I don't. I've never given my dog a bath.

6. A. Do you like to eat sushi?
   B. Of course! I've eaten sushi for many years.

7. A. I just got a big raise! Did you also get one?
   B. Actually, I've never gotten a raise.

8. A. I did very well on the math exam. How about you?
   B. I've never done well on a math exam.

Page 47 Exercise O

What things have these people done? What haven't they done? Listen and check Yes or No.

1. A. Carla, have you done your homework yet?
   B. Yes, I have. I did my homework this morning.
   A. And have you practiced the violin?
   B. No, I haven't practiced yet. I promise I'll practice this afternoon.

2. A. Kevin?
   B. Yes, Mrs. Blackwell?
   A. Have you written your report yet?
   B. No, I haven't. I'll write it immediately.
   A. And have you sent a fax to the Crane Company?
   B. No, I haven't. I promise I'll send them a fax after I write the report.

3. A. Have you fed the dog yet?
   B. Yes, I have. I fed him a few minutes ago.
   A. Good. Well, I guess we can leave for work now.
   B. But we haven't eaten breakfast yet!

4. A. I'm leaving now, Mr. Green.
   B. Have you fixed the pipes in the basement, Charlie?
   A. Yes, I have.
   B. And have you repaired the washing machine?
   A. Yes, I have. It's working again.
   B. That's great! Thank you, Charlie.
   A. I'll send you a bill, Mr. Green.

5. A. You know, we haven't done the laundry all week.
   B. I know. We should do it today.
   A. We also haven't vacuumed the rugs!
   B. We haven't?
   A. No, we haven't.
   B. Oh. I guess we should vacuum them today.

6. A. Are we ready for the party?
   B. I think so. We've gotten all the food at the supermarket, and we've cleaned the house from top to bottom!
   A. Well, I guess we're ready for the party!

7. A. Have you spoken to the landlord about our broken light?
   B. Yes, I have. I spoke to him this morning.
   A. What did he say?
   B. He said we should call an electrician.
   A. Okay. Let's call Ajax Electric.
   B. Don't worry. I've already called them, and they're coming this afternoon.

8. A. Have you hooked up the new VCR yet?
   B. I can't do it. It's really difficult.
   A. Have you read the instructions?
   B. Yes, I have. I've read them ten times, and I still can't understand them!

Page 56 Exercise E

Listen and choose the correct answer.

1. Bob has been engaged since he got out of the army.
2. My sister Carol has been a professional musician since she finished music school.
3. Michael has been home since he fell and hurt himself last week.
4. My wife has gotten up early every morning since she started her new job.
5. Richard has eaten breakfast in the school cafeteria every morning since he started college.
6. Nancy and Tom have known each other for five and a half years.
7. My friend Charlie and I have played soccer every weekend since we were eight years old.
8. Patty has had short hair since she was a teenager.
9. Ron has owned his own business since he moved to Chicago nine years ago.
10. I've been interested in astronomy for the past eleven years.
11. I use my personal computer all the time. I've had it since I was in high school.
12. Alan has had problems with his house since he bought it fifteen years ago.

Page 61 Exercise L

Listen and choose the correct answer.

1. A. Have you always been a salesperson?
   B. No. I've been a salesperson for the past four years. Before that, I was a cashier.

2. A. How long has your daughter been in medical school?
   B. She's been in medical school for the past two years.

3. A. Have your parents always lived in a house?
   B. No. They've lived in a house for the past ten years. Before that, they lived in an apartment.

4. A. How long have you wanted to be an actor?
   B. I've wanted to be an actor since I was in college. Before that, I wanted to be a musician.

5. A. Do you and your husband still exercise at your health club every day?
   B. No. We haven't done that for a year.

6. A. Has James been a bachelor all his life?
   B. No, he hasn't. He was married for ten years.

7. A. Has your sister Jane always wanted to be a writer?
   B. Yes, she has. She's wanted to be a writer all her life.

8. A. Have you ever broken your ankle?
   B. No. I've sprained it a few times, but I've never broken it.

9. A. Have you always liked classical music?
   B. No. I've liked classical music for the past few years. Before that, I liked rock music.

10. A. Has Billy had a sore throat for a long time?
    B. He's had a sore throat for the past two days. Before that, he had a fever.

11. A. Jennifer has been the store manager since last fall.
    B. What did she do before that?
    A. She was a salesperson.

12. A. Have you always been interested in modern art?
    B. No. I've been interested in modern art since I moved to Paris a few years ago. Before that, I was only interested in sports.

Page 64 Exercise E

Listen and choose the correct time expressions to complete the sentences.

1. A. How long have you been living there?
   B. I've been living there since . . .
2. A. How long has your daughter been practicing the piano?
   B. She's been practicing for . . .
3. A. How long have I been running?
   B. You've been running since . . .
4. A. How long have you been feeling bad?
   B. I've been feeling bad for . . .
5. A. How long have they been waiting?
   B. They've been waiting for . . .
6. A. How long has your son been studying?
   B. He's been studying since . . .
7. A. How long have your sister and her boyfriend been dating?
   B. They've been dating since . . .
8. A. Dad, how long have we been driving?
   B. Hmm. I think we've been driving for . . .
9. A. How long has your little girl been crying?
   B. She's been crying for . . .

Page 67 Exercise H

Listen and choose what the people are talking about.

1. She's been directing it for an hour.
2. We've been rearranging it all morning.
3. I've been paying them on time.
4. He's been playing them for years.
5. Have you been bathing them for a long time?
6. They've been rebuilding it for a year.
7. She's been writing it for a week.
8. He's been translating them for many years.
9. I've been reading it all afternoon.
10. She's been knitting them for a few weeks.
11. We've been listening to them all afternoon.
12. I've been recommending it for years.
13. They've been repairing it all day.
14. She's been taking it all morning.
15. I've been solving them all my life.

Page 71 Exercise L

Listen and decide where the conversation is taking place.

1. A. I'm really tired.
   B. No wonder! You've been chopping tomatoes for the past hour.
2. A. Mark! I'm surprised. You've been falling asleep in class all morning, and you've never fallen asleep in class before.
   B. I'm sorry, Mrs. Applebee. It won't happen again.
3. A. I've been washing these shirts for the past half hour, and they still aren't clean.
   B. Here. Try this Presto Soap.
4. A. We've been standing in line for an hour and forty-five minutes.
   B. I know. I hope the movie is good. I've never stood in line for such a long time.

5. A. What seems to be the problem, Mr. Jones?
   B. My back has been hurting me for the past few days.
   A. I'm sorry to hear that.
6. A. You know, we've been reading here for more than two hours.
   B. You're right. I think it's time to go now.
7. A. Do you want to leave?
   B. I think so. We've seen all the paintings here.
8. A. How long have you been exercising?
   B. For an hour and a half.
9. A. We've been waiting for an hour, and it still isn't here.
   B. I know. I'm going to be late for work.
10. A. I think we've seen them all. Which one do you want to buy?
    B. I like that black one over there.
11. A. We've been watching this movie for the past hour, and it's terrible!
    B. You're right. Let's change the channel.
12. A. I've got a terrible headache.
    B. Why?
    A. Customers have been complaining all morning.
    B. What have they been complaining about?
    A. Some people have been complaining about our terrible products, but most people have been complaining about our high prices.

Page 77 Exercise F

Listen and choose the correct answer.

1. A. How long has Janet been an actress?
   B. She's been an actress since she graduated from acting school.
2. A. Have you watched the news yet?
   B. Yes. I saw the president, and I heard his speech.
3. A. Have you always lived in Denver?
   B. No. We've lived in Denver since 1995. Before that, we lived in New York.
4. A. Has Dad made dinner yet?
   B. Not yet. He still has to make it.
5. A. How long has your ceiling been leaking?
   B. It's been leaking for more than a week.
   A. Have you called the superintendent?
   B. Yes, I have. I've called him several times.
6. A. Billy is having trouble with his homework.
   B. Has he asked anyone to help him?
   A. No, he hasn't.

Page 87 Exercise N

Listen and choose the correct answer.

1. Dr. Gomez really enjoys . . .
2. Whenever possible, my wife and I try to avoid . . .
3. Next summer I'm going to learn . . .
4. Every day Rita practices . . .
5. My parents have decided . . .
6. I've considered . . .
7. Are you thinking about . . .
8. I'm going to quit . . .
9. Why do you keep on . . .
10. My doctor says I should stop . . .
11. David can't stand . . .
12. Are you going to continue to . . .

(continued)

13. James doesn't want to start . . .
14. Next semester Kathy is going to begin . . .
15. You know, you can't keep on . . .

Page 97 Exercise J
Listen and choose the correct answer.

1. Steve lost his voice.
2. Is Beverly one of your relatives?
3. We just canceled our trip to South America.
4. Ricky has been failing all of his tests this year.
5. Francine dislocated her shoulder.
6. What did you and your students discuss in class?
7. My girlfriend and I rode on the roller coaster yesterday.
8. Grandma can't chew this piece of steak very well.
9. Jimmy loves my homemade food.
10. Did you see the motorcycles go by?
11. Do you think Mr. Montero will take a day off soon?
12. Amy wanted to ask her boss for a raise, but she got cold feet.
13. Have you heard that Margaret sprained her wrist?
14. I have to make an important decision.
15. I envy you.
16. I feel terrible. Debbie and Dan broke up last week.
17. My ankle hurts a lot.
18. I was heartbroken when I heard what happened.
19. Michael was furious with his neighbors.
20. We went to a recital last night.
21. Tom, don't forget to shine your shoes!
22. My friend Carla is extremely athletic.
23. My husband and I have been writing invitations all afternoon.
24. Charles rented a beautiful tuxedo for his niece's wedding.

Page 99 Exercise D
Listen and choose the correct answer.

Ex. My grandfather likes to . . .
1. Susan says she's going to stop . . .
2. My wife and I are thinking about . . .
3. David is considering . . .
4. I can't stand to . . .
5. You should definitely keep on . . .

Page 105 Exercise G
Listen and choose the correct answer.

1. A. I looked in the refrigerator, and I can't find the orange juice.
   B. That's because we . . .

2. A. I'm frustrated! My computer isn't working today.
   B. I think you forgot to . . .

3. A. What should I do with the Christmas decorations?
   B. I think it's time to . . .

4. A. Should I take these clothes to the cleaner's?
   B. Yes. You should definitely . . .

5. A. Hmm. What does this word mean?
   B. You should . . .

6. A. I have to return this skateboard to my cousin.
   B. When are you going to . . . ?

7. A. This math problem is very difficult.
   B. Maybe I can . . .

8. A. I'll never remember their new telephone number.
   B. You should . . .

9. A. I just spilled milk on the kitchen floor!
   B. Don't worry. I'll . . .

Page 108 Exercise L
Listen and choose the correct answer.

1. I really look up to my father.
2. My brother picks on me all the time.
3. Did you throw away the last can of paint?
4. I still haven't gotten over the flu.
5. Have you heard from your cousin Sam recently?
6. Why did you turn him down?
7. Did your French teacher call on you today?
8. George picked out a new suit for his wedding.
9. I have to drop my sister off at the airport.
10. Everything in the store is 20 percent off this week.
11. This jacket fits you.
12. Did you try on a lot of shoes?

Page 112 Exercise D
Listen and complete the sentences.

1. I missed the bus this morning.
2. I'm allergic to nuts.
3. I'll be on vacation next week.
4. I've never flown in a helicopter.
5. I can speak Chinese.
6. I like to go sailing.
7. I'm not going to the company picnic this weekend.
8. I saw a very good movie last night.
9. I don't go on many business trips.
10. I've been to London several times.
11. I'm not a vegetarian.
12. I should lose a little weight.
13. I can't stop worrying about my health.
14. I hate to drive downtown.
15. I won't be able to go to Nancy's party this Saturday night.

Page 117 Exercise K
Listen and complete the sentences.

1. I missed the bus today, . . .
2. I'm allergic to cats, . . .
3. I'll be on vacation next week, . . .
4. You've never seen a rainbow, . . .
5. I can speak Italian, . . .
6. I like to go sailing, . . .
7. I've been on television several times, . . .
8. I saw an exciting movie last weekend, . . .
9. I won't be in the office tomorrow, . . .
10. We were late, . . .
11. I'm not a vegetarian, . . .
12. I saw the stop sign, . . .
13. I can't swim very well, . . .
14. They have to work overtime this weekend, . . .
15. I won't be able to go to Sam's party this Friday night, . . .
16. I'm not afraid of flying, . . .
17. I haven't eaten breakfast yet, . . .
18. The other students weren't bored, . . .

Page 121 Exercise C
Listen and complete the sentences.

Ex. Nancy knows how to type, . . .
1. I'm interested in science, . . .
2. I won't be home this evening, . . .
3. I own my own business, . . .
4. I've never hooked up a computer, . . .
5. You just got a raise, . . .

Correlation Key

Student Text Pages	Activity Workbook Pages	Student Text Pages	Activity Workbook Pages
Chapter 1		**Chapter 7**	
2	2–3	82	78–79
3	4–5	84	80–81
4	6–8	86–87	82
7–8	9–11	88–89	83–84
Chapter 2		90–91	85–87
12	12–13	**Chapter 8**	
13	14–17	96–97	88–89
14–15	18–19	100	90
18–19	20–23	101	91
Chapter 3		104–105	92–93
22–23	24–26	106–107	94–96
25	27	109	97
26	28–29	**Check-Up Test**	**98–99**
27	30	**Gazette**	**99a–d**
28–29	31–33	**Chapter 9**	
Check-Up Test	**34–35**	116	100
Gazette	**35a–d**	117	101–102
Chapter 4		119	103
38	36	122–123	104–105
39	37	124	106–107
40	38	126–127	108
41	39	**Chapter 10**	
42–43	40–43	132	109–110
45	44–45	133	111–112
46	46–47	134–135	113
48	48–50	138–139	114–115
50	51	141	116–117
Chapter 5		143	118–119
52–53	52–54	**Check-Up Test**	**120–121**
56–57	55–57	**Gazette**	**121a–c**
58–59	58–59		
62–63	60–61		
Gazette	**61a–d**		
Chapter 6			
70–71	62–65		
72	66–68		
74–75	69–71		
76–77	72–75		
Check-Up Test	**76–77**		

SIDE *by* SIDE *Extra* Activity Workbook Audio Program

The *Side by Side Extra* Activity Workbook Digital Audio CDs contain all Workbook listening activities and GrammarRaps for entertaining language practice through rhythm, stress, and intonation. Students can use the Audio Program to extend their language learning through self-study outside the classroom. The Digital Audio CDs also include MP3 files of the audio program for downloading to a computer or audio player.

Audio Program Contents